The **25**-Day
Money Makeover
for **Women**

The 25-Day
Money Makeover
for Women

Francine L. Huff

SPIRE

© 2004 by Francine L. Huff

Published by Fleming H. Revell
a division of Baker Publishing Group
P.O. Box 6287, Grand Rapids, MI 49516-6287
www.revellbooks.com

Spire edition published 2006
ISBN 10: 0-8007-8743-9
ISBN 978-0-8007-8743-1

Second printing, March 2007

Previously published in 2004 under the title *The 25-Day Financial Makeover*

Printed in the United States of America

All rights reserved. No part of this publication may be reproduced, stored in a retrieval system, or transmitted in any form or by any means—for example, electronic, photocopy, recording—without the prior written permission of the publisher. The only exception is brief quotations in printed reviews.

Unless otherwise indicated, Scripture is taken from the HOLY BIBLE, NEW INTERNATIONAL VERSION®. NIV®. Copyright © 1973, 1978, 1984 by International Bible Society. Used by permission of Zondervan. All rights reserved.

This publication is designed to provide accurate and authoritative information. It is sold with the understanding that neither the author nor the publisher is engaged in rendering legal, investment, accounting, or other professional services. If expert assistance is required, the services of a competent professional person should be sought.

To Gregory

Contents

Introduction

Getting people to organize and clean up their finances can be like pulling teeth. It hurts! Often it becomes easier to avoid reining in out-of-control habits and behavior than to accept the call to responsible stewardship. At prayer time many folks earnestly ask God to show them the path away from their money woes and to bless them overwhelmingly and abundantly. But somewhere along the way they don't do *their* part toward achieving that goal. "I'm just gonna wait on Jesus for a big ol' miracle," they tell family and friends, while waiting for him to do all the work.

As a young newspaper reporter right out of college, I learned to live frugally on my modest paycheck. I was able to cover rent, basic living expenses, student loan payments, and little more. My immature handling of a credit card during college resulted in me beginning my adult working life with a blot on my credit record. Because I couldn't get another card for several years, I only bought things when I had enough cash. You would think this set up a pattern for responsible money management that carried over as my income grew, right? Wrong!

After changing jobs a few years later and being blessed with a higher salary, I began to feast on the material possessions I felt I had been denied for several years, such as a new stereo and computer. While I genuinely needed some of the things I purchased, often I was shopping just to pass the time. Once the credit card offers began pouring into my mailbox, I wasted no time joining the ranks of America's debt-plagued consumers.

Frustration over having little savings and the constant stress of keeping up with my credit card bills finally snapped me out of my buying binge. My prayers to get out of financial quicksand became more genuine and led to some critical self-assessment. When I read Proverbs 17:16—"Of what use is money in the hand of a fool, since he has no desire to get wisdom?"—a light bulb went on in my head. I had been acting like a fool, throwing away money on things I really didn't need and focusing too much on keeping up appearances. I was angry with myself and ashamed that I'd abused the resources God had given me.

I was a young Christian who was just beginning to understand the concept of applying biblical principles to *all* areas of my life. Hungry to learn more, I searched for what God had to say on the subject of money and possessions, and I began to understand that my spending was linked only partly to a desire for material possessions.

Shopping gave me an outlet for the feelings of loneliness and isolation I felt because I was living far away from my family and most of my friends. It was easy to go to the mall, even if I didn't have a friend to shop with. And if I looked good in new clothes and had a fabulous hairdo, I thought, surely I'd be able to get a date and would no longer have to be lonely. Addressing the feelings of loneliness helped bring healing to other areas of my life. I began to curb my out-of-control spending and deal with my time alone much better.

"But Jesus often withdrew to lonely places and prayed" (Luke 5:16). Even though the environment Jesus lived in was different from our modern world, it had its own distractions. He knew the benefits of having time alone, whether in the wilderness or in a boat. After those periods of solitude, he would emerge refreshed and ready to continue with his calling.

As my appreciation grew for my times of solitude and for the possibilities of what I could accomplish, I relied less on shopping trips and other activities that got me deeper in debt. Exercising, volunteering, and other free or low-cost activities filled up more of my time, and my home became a haven and retreat. But just as important, solid plans for managing money, paying off debt, and saving up for a home were formed, and I began studying personal finance books and magazines. Now I continue to remind myself that I'm just the caretaker of what the Creator has allowed me to have.

Do you know what motivates your spending? Are you willing to admit that there are influences and patterns in your life that are keeping you in debt, living paycheck to paycheck, or unsure about how you're going to meet your family's basic needs? Are you interested in assessing the difference between wants and needs? Perhaps some of the poor financial habits learned from your own parents are keeping you in fear and bondage.

Just as the goal of a beauty makeover is to help you look, smell, and feel pretty, this 25-day makeover will help get rid of some of your financial junk—and for a whole lot less than a visit to the salon. Many women spend lots of time and money in beauty salons and day spas. Being pampered can make even the most stressed-out woman feel like a princess for a day. But the rosy glow is usually long forgotten by the time the credit card bills for all those wonderful manicures, perms, and facials show up in the mailbox. If you haven't done so before, you owe it to yourself to invest in a makeover that will not only make you feel good, but will teach you positive financial habits that will last a lifetime.

Women are increasingly flexing their financial muscle and becoming bigger players in the global economy, and almost half the U.S. workforce is female. According to the U.S. Census Bureau, the median income of women working full time rose to $31,223 in 2004. As that group's spending power continues to increase, it's no wonder that corporate America is looking to court these consumers. Mortgage lenders, auto companies, financial-planning professionals, and home improvement specialists are all trying to grab a piece of the pie by offering more products and services targeted specifically at women. But with the smorgasbord of opportunities and advice being presented, trying to discern the right financial path to follow can be confusing.

Many people look to those around them for cues on what to do with their money. But think about it: As much as you love and care about them, why would you take financial advice from your family and friends if they aren't any better (and are possibly worse) at managing their own resources? Take the time to educate yourself and set up a financial management system that works for your household. Once you begin making changes, don't be surprised if the people in your life start coming to *you* for advice in this area. Being a good steward over your resources will begin to positively impact you as well as others in your sphere of influence. When that happens, don't hold it over their heads, but share it in humility.

Gaining control over your money begins with taking a step back and evaluating with an honest and open heart exactly where you and your money stand. Are you intimidated by the thought of confronting this area of your life? Perhaps you just go around saying *que sera, sera* ("whatever will be, will be") and are resigned to always being broke and stressed about money matters. Maybe you take a more passive approach and keep hoping your financial mess will eventually disappear. Or maybe you keep dreaming of the day you hit it big at the casino or in the lottery. If you know that your spending is out of control and you're not making good fiscal decisions, then continuing to be in denial or having unrealistic expectations won't solve the problem.

The 25-Day Money Makeover for Women will help you confront some of the issues that may be holding you back from better managing your money and other resources. Not everyone has the same view of money or needs, but most of us can use some help organizing our finances. If you're looking for a get-rich-quick fix to your financial woes, this is not the book for you. But if you're looking for some realistic, godly steps you can apply to take control of your situation and continue using for years to come, then keep reading.

I am not a financial planner, but I have had many opportunities to speak with a variety of women—both professionally as a journalist and personally—who've indicated a hunger for a manageable system for organizing and managing money. Many of them know they should get rid of debt but don't understand *why* they continue to spend. They know they should save and pick good investments but aren't sure *how* to choose them. They know the Bible talks about money but aren't really sure *what* it says. Like many of these women, I've learned some financial lessons the hard way. But I made a conscious choice to change poor financial habits and to implement a workable system of managing money instead of letting money manage me.

The steps in this book can be implemented over a 25-day period and are meant to be a beginning for positive lifetime habits. Don't worry if you skip a day here and there or don't complete everything in exactly twenty-five days. Depending on your age or family situation, some of the chapters may be more involved than others or may not apply as much to your situation. In some cases you may have to wait for information you requested to be mailed to you before completing a task. But if you do miss a day, get back to the plan as soon as possible so you can establish good habits and reach your financial goals sooner.

Each chapter of this book has Scriptures, assignments, and prayers to assist you on your walk. Really think about the questions being asked and answer them honestly. You will find it helpful to keep a journal to record your progress as you go through this book. After you've completed the tasks outlined in each chapter, take time to write down how you feel about the area that you've addressed. Even if your finances are in total chaos, remember that the Lord loves you and is a forgiving God. And if he knows you're applying his wisdom and can forgive you for making a complete mess of the resources he's given you, then who are you to keep beating up on yourself? Now, let's get ready for a financial makeover!

How Do You Feel about Money?

Your word is a lamp to my feet and a light for my path.

Psalm 119:105

Walk into a room full of people, begin talking about money, and the chances are pretty good that a variety of strong emotions will be stirred up. Some people may feel smug and satisfied that they have a big income and have "made it" according to the world's standards. Others might feel melancholy or anxious because they haven't figured out how to stretch their hard-earned paychecks to cover all the material possessions society says they should want and have. Some in the room may be relieved they have just enough to cover their bills and debts, but aren't really sure where they're heading beyond that. A few folks might leave, hoping you won't ask to borrow any money from them!

> Get to know your own beliefs and opinions about money and its place in your life. Using a four-step plan, establish your personal financial goals.

With mixed messages being circulated throughout society about money and possessions, it's easy to get sucked into the whirlwind of buying more stuff. Obtaining fancier cars, designer clothing, and the latest electronics consumes more and more time, as does getting the credit to purchase them. Instead of working to serve God and finding fulfillment in his kingdom, many people become slaves to earning their next dollar just to stay ahead. So much energy gets focused on paying bills and buying more stuff that often there is little left over to enjoy family, friends, or activities that are really of interest. High anxiety, physical ailments, and other bad habits may follow. In some cases, tired, stressed-out people turn to second or even third jobs in order to maintain their extravagant lifestyles.

Men and women both face anxieties over money, but not always for the same reasons. "Men will be depressed and be unfulfilled in their jobs and relationships and say they have to be the breadwinner. That makes them more stressed, and they go out and buy themselves something bright, shiny and new—boy toys," says Dr. Anita Thomas, associate professor of counselor education at Northeastern Illinois University in Chicago. The threat of layoffs combined with overall lower savings rates has resulted in more Americans shopping to make themselves feel better, even if they can't afford it.

The stress women feel about money is often tied to issues of independence, says Thomas, who also does mental health counseling at her church. Articles and books tell women to have financial independence, especially in case the husband dies, and that puts too much pressure on women to maintain a career along with their other family responsibilities. That pressure can lead to buying sprees.

"I think a lot of women have stress that purchases should be equal, so they can have a stake and a claim. They don't want the house to get divided and then they end up with nothing," says Thomas. And because a lot of the male gender identity is caught up in being the primary earner, that focus on achieving independence creates a double bind for men and women and can ultimately be hurtful to a marriage by causing a tug-of-war over money, a leading cause of divorce (Eph. 5:28–30).

Thomas's holistic approach gets clients to address their fiscal problems in relation to other areas, including their emotional, physical, and psychological states. "It makes them realize that financial issues have a bigger role in their everyday life than they may realize," she says. For couples, sitting down, discussing their concerns, and working out a budget and a financial plan can help with other troubled areas of their relationship. Singles can confront fears or uncertainty about the future by taking a hard look at how much of a financial cushion they would have if they lost their job or had an emergency. Often stepping back to look at the big picture will put things in true perspective and help diminish feelings of panic.

God's Ownership

If you're having money problems, stop and ask yourself: Who am I trying to impress? Do I really need all this stuff I buy, or am I just stuck on the belief that I deserve to have it? Do I even know *why* I crave bigger and better things?

How important is money to my life? Why can't I be content with what I have?

If you don't know the answer to some or all of these questions, then you don't have a clear idea of your personal financial goals. Your coworkers and neighbors can't give you clarity in this area and may only confuse you further. You need to follow God's Word when making fiscal decisions. He's the true owner of our possessions and has only given them to us to use and enjoy. "Through him all things were made; without him nothing was made that has been made" (John 1:3). We must accept his ownership before we can truly become good managers of those resources and receive all the blessings he has for us, as Jesus explains in the parable of the steward who squandered his master's possessions (Luke 16:1–15).

Nevertheless, many people struggle with the concept of God's ownership and being responsible for their own financial choices. "I'm trying to live the belief that the money I have honestly belongs to God. But at the moment when I see something I want I'm not thinking that way," says Faith, 36, who says she lets her husband handle their finances and avoids most money issues. "It's trying to bring my heart around what my mind knows. I don't think I'm honestly an adult when it comes to money."

A college-educated woman who says she has a good understanding of money and investing, Faith says she's just not that interested in keeping track of the household expenses. She says her parents and grandparents provided good examples of money management while she was growing up, but no one ever talked about money. "In the late '70s my father made $100,000 a year, but I had no idea how that fit with anything," she says. "I leave everything in my husband's hands . . . I don't respect my position on finances. However, I'm not doing a lot to change it."

Faith's internal conflict may strike a familiar chord in your life. If you, too, are having trouble accepting your adult role as a caretaker of God's belongings, try spending more time in prayer, meditation, and Bible study. "I'm trying to control impulsive spending more. Before I get out of my car, I try to say a prayer and remind myself where I want to be [spiritually and financially]," Faith says. "My goal financially is just to be mature about what I have, whether it's a lot or a little, and to handle it in the way the Bible tells us we should handle it."

By overspending as God's children, we are telling him that we know better than he does how our money should be spent. We are telling him that we are lord over our finances. Repentance is key to breaking free from this pride.

The Role of Money

To establish workable financial goals, you must first determine exactly what role money plays in your life, using the four-step process in figure 1.1. First, determine what matters most to you and what you want to accomplish. Is it more quality time with your family? A six-figure income and accolades from your peers? Learning to be content with what you have? Making a difference in the world? Being financially comfortable enough to follow your calling into full-time ministry? Homeschooling your children and being a stay-at-home mom?

Steps to Setting Goals

1. List life goals and beliefs.
2. Does behavior support or contradict goals?
3. List specific financial goals.
4. Form action plan to surmount obstacles.

Figure 1.1

Whatever system of beliefs and values you have should be listed in your journal under the heading "Important Life Goals." It may help to think of it this way: If you knew you had only one year to live, what would be most important to you and how would you spend your time? List as many ideas as you feel apply to your situation. If you really believe that working ten hours a day in corporate America is the ultimate goal in your life, then by all means list it. However, I suspect that item won't grace most people's list!

The second step is to read through that list again. Ask yourself these two questions: Do my present fiscal habits move me closer to or further away from this goal? Am I willing to make sacrifices to get where I want to be financially? If you wrote down that you want to give money to charitable organizations but are currently giving zero in this area and are instead filling your closet with clothing you don't need, then your current spending is incompatible with that life goal. If you find that many of the life goals you stated aren't supported by your financial habits, then it's time to reprioritize some things and create a new action plan.

Write down how you feel about your overall financial situation under the heading "My Feelings." You may be pretty comfortable with where you are or somewhat stunned to realize how wide apart your life goals and current financial habits are. Your honesty is crucial to achieving success with your makeover and moving past any fears and bondage you may have. What you write is between you and the Creator, so try not to avoid serious issues that you know are hanging over your life.

If you make a good income but gamble much of it away every month, then you need to get with God and deal with that. Stop joining in the office lottery-ticket pool if that's a temptation. If you're losing sleep at night because you're a single parent and are struggling to make ends meet and purchase a home, take it to God in prayer. Ask for clarity about your financial picture as well as other areas of your life and what he wants you to achieve. Ask for forgiveness for wasting or mismanaging resources and for the wisdom you need to heal your finances.

The third step for establishing financial goals will provide a blueprint for daily decision making and transactions. Just as an architect draws a blueprint to be used when building a house, your plan will help build a stronger foundation for your fiscal habits. Think about what specific needs or wants you have and list them under the heading "Financial Goals." If you've been struggling to pay for your child's education or praying that you and your husband will come to better agreement over money matters, then list that here. Remember, be realistic with your plans. Becoming a millionaire in a month is not a realistic goal.

Step four is determining what the biggest obstacles are to achieving the financial goals on your list and developing at least one action plan to surmount them. List those under the heading "Obstacles and Action Plan." For example, is the real issue that you haven't received a raise in five years or that you've been mismanaging your funds? If mismanaging your money is the issue, then write down: "I will begin managing my money better starting NOW!" Perhaps a steady paycheck has kept you tied to the same job for years without any real sense of purpose or fulfillment. If so, then perhaps you need to write: "I will look for a new job that fulfills me and moves me closer to my life goals."

The Berlin Wall, built in 1961 to separate communist East Berlin from the noncommunist western half of the city, kept people trapped and cut off from relatives and friends for almost thirty years. Many died trying to escape over the wall, which came to represent a symbol of oppression throughout the world. In 1989 border crossings were opened, and by October 1990 when East and West Germany reunited as one free country, the massive wall was being torn down.[1] The joy and relief that citizens on both sides of the city—as well as throughout the entire country—must have felt upon seeing the 26-mile-long wall topple is hard to imagine.

Even before the government officially began tearing down the barrier, reports circulated of excited Germans celebrating by climbing up and hammering off pieces of the wall, as the following excerpt from an article in the German newspaper *Die Welt* describes.

> At the south end of the Hindenburg Platz, where the Wall is 3.5 metres tall, the sounds of hammers were heard for hours. The young people succeeded at breaking off some of the round concrete blocks, and dropping them over into the death strip in the East. As dawn arrived one of the upper parts of a concrete plate reinforced with steel broke off, amid much cheering.[2]

However big or small your obstacles may be, it's time to get a sledge hammer and strike them down. Don't remain cut off from the blessings God has waiting for you in his kingdom. Pray to be released from the grip of fear or self-doubt that may be keeping you paralyzed and unable to make changes in your life.

Prayer Box
Lord, help me to be a good steward of the money and resources you've given me. Please break my willful spirit and use me as the caretaker you've called me to be. I know that being a good manager requires facing up to any misconceptions and fears I may have. Help me to find a sense of purpose and to manage my finances in a way that will bring me closer to that and relieve some of the stress I feel. Please give me the strength to confront the obstacles that have kept me from my goals. I want to be a faithful, responsible, and humble servant. Amen.

Track Your Spending

Now we know that whatever the law says, it says to those
who are under the law, so that every mouth may be silenced
and the whole world held accountable to God.

Romans 3:19

Many mornings as I headed to work, I would stop
and purchase a cup of coffee to drink on my com-
mute. Settling into my seat on the train with the
hot java—preferably chocolate raspberry or hazelnut—and
my morning newspapers was a comfortable and satisfying
ritual. The $1 to $1.50 tab I ran up each morning, depending on where I bought the coffee, barely registered with me.
After all, $5 to $6 a week for a morning cup of coffee isn't
very much, and I wasn't buying the fancy lattes and more
expensive drinks.

But after getting into the habit of making coffee at home
to take with me, I found that at the end of each week I'd
have more money in my wallet. That extra change began to
add up, and I found myself hitting the ATM less frequently.

After doing the math, I realized that if I bought coffee once a day for five days, that added up to at least $260 a year. That doesn't seem like much, does it? After all, $260 doesn't really buy all that much in today's economy, you might be thinking. Well, not much more than about a year's premium on a life insurance policy for a healthy, nonsmoking, forty-year-old woman . . . or a new exercise

> **Identify your spending patterns by keeping track of all your expenses. Make a firm commitment to implement positive changes in your financial habits.**

bike to help stay fit . . . or a continuing-education class at a local community college. . . . Get the picture?

Small purchases like coffee may not seem like much at first, but when you look at the long term you get a better appreciation for what's being spent. (By the way, that $260 figure doesn't take into account other drinks, snacks, or lunches I might occasionally purchase throughout my workday.) Eventually I realized I had to be accountable at all times for how I was spending my money. Taking coffee from home and packing a lunch started looking better and better—and became easier as time passed.

It's the Little Stuff

While spending a dollar here and there may seem like a small thing, it really does add up to a lot of dough when you factor in all the impulse purchases that can happen throughout the course of just one day. Buying that granola bar for an afternoon snack, those cute little earrings you saw in a boutique near the office, or that sweater you know will look so adorable on your daughter can wreak havoc on household finances when they aren't being tracked. Perhaps some of your excess spending is going toward habits that you're better off breaking anyway. For instance, not only is smoking bad for your health, but with cigarette prices around $5 a pack it can put a huge strain on your wallet.

Do you know how much money you're spending each day? Or do you take money out of the ATM, toss the receipt in the trash, and then wonder where on earth all that cash went? Maybe you're waiting for your husband to balance the checkbook. It's his turn anyway. . . .

Keeping close tabs on daily purchasing habits will allow you to nip some of that spending in the bud and find more money for things such as paying down debt, dance lessons for the kids, or live music at your wedding. Think about what is driving your impulse purchases. Lisa, 24, says she bought a dress she really didn't need because it was a real bargain at $3. "The only problem was they didn't have any in my size," she says. "I bought it anyway. I have to wear high-heeled boots that hurt my feet (I got them on clearance, too!) and safety pin the shoulders to my bra straps to keep it from sliding too far forward."

Often people buy small things as a treat to themselves because they have stress-filled lives that leave little time for relaxation. They justify spending $5 on a trinket that's not really needed because it makes them feel better. The emotional high and sense of accomplishment that may accompany the purchase can be enough to temporarily erase the memory of losing sleep the previous night over not having enough money for the next month's rent.

If you know that you're consistently using impulse purchases to dull the pain in other areas of your life, then make a choice to say enough. Be accountable to yourself and to God by making a conscious effort not to buy things you really don't need. Ask his forgiveness for placing too much emphasis on material possessions and for making poor financial decisions to obtain them.

If you know that you will have trouble refraining from impulse purchases, find a relative or female friend to whom you can be accountable. Perhaps she's struggling with some of the same issues and you can pray for each other. This accountability partner is not someone who should beat you up every time you spend a dollar, but should instead be an encourager who will support you through difficult times and temptations. You can then support her in the same way. Perhaps you can both work through this book separately and then share what you've learned.

Other than a husband or close male relative, I recommend women avoid partnering with men to keep from mixing finances with other emotions that may be present. If you're confused about this, watch a couple episodes of *The People's Court* or any other courtroom TV show in which a large percentage of the cases revolve around women being taken advantage of financially by men with whom they were romantically involved.

Once you've decided to be responsible for your fiscal choices, it's time to begin tracking daily expenses. By writing down all of your spending habits for a month, you'll get a comprehensive picture of where your money is going. Fixed expenses such as housing, utilities, and loan payments don't fluctuate too much from month to month. But if you do find that certain expenses such as telephone and electricity services are gyrating each month, you may want to look into fixed payment plans that are offered by many utilities, or set your own limits on how many long distance calls you'll make each month.

Keeping track of all expenses may seem like a pain in the beginning, and you may forget to record some purchases.

But as with making any kind of substantial change, you must discipline yourself to follow through with this step of your 25-day makeover. Just as you may take the time each day to apply makeup, fix your hair, or floss in order to look good, this process will advance the ultimate goal of sprucing up your finances.

If you have a spouse or live in a household with other adult family members, ask them to track their expenses, too, to get the most complete snapshot of your family's spending. They may resist doing this, but you should continue forward with your personal goal of better stewardship and pray for them to come to a better understanding of how important this task is.

A Living Example

Just because you've made a decision to be a better manager of your money doesn't mean that others around you will understand this or take your efforts seriously. In fact, don't be surprised if you encounter resentment from some people because you are making a genuine effort to change and take authority over this area of your life. They may be skeptical of your desire to change or even fearful that you will move beyond a shared comfort zone of poor fiscal behavior and bad habits. But if you're faithful in your pursuit of God's blessings and become disciplined with your money, your actions will speak louder than any words. When you do have to speak to them about this issue, "Let your conversation be always full of grace, seasoned with salt, so that you may know how to answer everyone" (Col. 4:6).

In *Becoming a Contagious Christian,* author Bill Hybels discusses the importance of authenticity in sharing one's faith. "Time and again, I've found that people are strongly drawn to sincerity. So it follows that one of the most important things you can do to effectively draw in friends and loved ones toward Christ is to simply be real. To avoid acting like more than you are or pretending you're less than what you are. To feel free, through the liberating power of God, to just be you."[1]

It's going to take work to get your finances in order, especially if you've been neglectful or just haven't learned how to make good choices. You may experience withdrawal because of having to deny yourself things. Spending can be an addiction. Friends may treat you differently. Maybe you can't associate with the same people at lunch because they like to shop afterward or talk about what they bought. Perhaps you will no longer be a "bank" in other people's lives because they won't be able to depend on borrowing money from you instead of being responsible themselves.

Changing your fiscal habits may also mean saying no to your coworkers' children's fundraisers and candy sales. Folks may misunderstand your motives or even get upset. But hopefully once any doubting Thomases see the transformation God is working in this area of your life, they'll respect you and become interested in making changes as well.

Ask the Father to give you joy regarding the changes you're making. Christ, for the joy set before him, did not reject the cross, but endured it (Heb. 12:2–3). Don't be discouraged by the small steps in your progress. You are running a race, so run to win. Keep your eyes on the prize and count it all joy when facing trials and tribulations.

Using the expense tracker shown in figure 2.1, write down each expense and the amount. Photocopy the worksheet and keep it in a folder that you designate for this, or glue it into your journal. If you have access to one of the financial software programs such as Quicken or Microsoft Money, you can use that to record your expenses. However, since most of us are unable to carry a computer everywhere we go (although handheld computers are changing this) it's easier to use copies of the worksheet or your journal. This task will take a lot of discipline and is best accomplished by carrying copies of the expense tracker with you each day. Do not neglect even the smallest purchases. Those packs of gum and highway tolls add up and are important pieces of your financial equation.

Always make sure you get a receipt for purchases. If you don't have time to record an expense when you make it, keep an envelope for the receipts in your purse, bag, or car. When you get home, be sure to add them to your expense tracker. Writing down how you feel when buying things will help you to see patterns in your spending. If you write "stressed and overwhelmed" every time you buy unhealthy snacks during your workday, then perhaps you'll need to find a better way to manage stress, such as going for a ten-minute walk or taking a prayer break.

The last column of the expense tracker allows you to note whether or not that expense was a need or a want. If you wrote a check for your mortgage or utilities, then you can easily determine those were financial needs. However, if you bought a new black dress but already have five other black dresses you've barely worn, then be honest with yourself that the purchase was really a want. At the end of each week, go back through your entries and look for any patterns in your feelings when you recorded expenses. Also, total up how much of your spending was a need versus a want. If, at the end of the month, your wants are totaling more than your needs, then you can see where the problems are and begin cutting back.

Expense Tracker

Date	Expense	Amount	Feelings	Need/Want?

Figure 2.1

If you're self-employed or get reimbursed by your employer for certain job-related expenses, documenting these items consistently throughout the year will make it easier for you at tax time. The Internal Revenue Service has guidelines for what expenses can be deducted on your tax form, and you should become familiar with which of those apply to your circumstances. But take care to keep receipts, cancelled checks, or other official statements to back up any deductions you claim.

Prayer Box

Lord, help me to be accountable for my spending each and every day. Help me to be honest about my wants and needs and not focus so much on acquiring unnecessary material possessions. I truly want to keep better tabs on where my money is going and what is motivating my buying habits. Please give me guidance and wisdom when making decisions about managing the resources I've been given. Amen.

**DAY
3**

Take a Look at Yourself

For the LORD gives wisdom, and from his mouth come knowledge and understanding.

Proverbs 2:6

Ignorance is bliss. What you don't know won't hurt you. Don't ask, don't tell.

These are just some of the catch phrases we hear that describe the process of looking the other way to avoid conflict. The idea is that many times it's better not to know or discuss information that might cause distress or undue embarrassment. However, when it comes to managing money, that concept just doesn't work if you're striving to be a good steward.

Do you confront controversy or problems head-on, determined to work out any complicated or unpleasant issues if you know that will ultimately benefit you? Or are you more likely to ignore facts staring you in the face because they make you feel uneasy?

> **Acknowledge responsibility for how your behavior has influenced your financial situation. Confront problems that need to be addressed and work on strategies to do this.**

Confronting the true state of our financial affairs can be uncomfortable, shocking, or even embarrassing. We may feel convicted that we haven't paid enough attention to the details or even acknowledged them. Information that may have been ignored is exposed, and we begin to feel a need to do something about it. That something may be sweeping financial dirt further under the rug and pretending everything is under control, or settling in for the long haul and doing the homework needed to clean up the mess.

Part of that homework is deciding that being fiscally responsible really is important to you, and not just because others say it should be. This includes looking at your situation without blinders and admitting the part *you* played in getting to your current financial status. Did you purposely pay your utility bills late for several months because you chose to spend money on entertainment with your friends? Perhaps you told a little white lie to your student loan company about some family emergency in order to get an extension on your payments.

Maybe you're thinking that you wouldn't even be in such dire financial straits if it weren't for the bad decisions or dishonest behavior of a spouse, family member, or friend. But even if this person's behavior does play a part in your current money woes, think about what role *you* played in allowing this to happen.

Did you continue giving your boyfriend money each time he wheedled it out of you because you were hoping it might convince him to go to church with you and commit to marriage? Or perhaps you knew your adult daughter wasn't making her car payments because it was more important for her to go out partying with her friends, but you decided it was easier to make them for her rather than deal with another argument. Really think about the choices you've made or the things you may have avoided doing rather than face a confrontation.

Look in the Mirror

It may be difficult to admit that your behavior isn't without flaws and may have been part of the problem. In fact, it may feel downright uncomfortable to admit that you've been blaming other people in your life for your poor decisions about money or that your codependent behavior allowed problems to escalate. But this humbling realization should remind you that you're only human and not perfect. "We all stumble in many ways. If anyone is never at fault in what he says, he is a perfect man, able to keep his whole body in check" (James 3:2).

Stopping codependent behavior can be especially difficult for married women, who've made a commitment to honor their husbands. "But honoring doesn't mean being stupid," says Trudy Colflesh, a licensed professional counselor in West Milford, New Jersey. "Submission means we equally submit to one another ... God doesn't intend for women to be manipulated and overpowered."

Colflesh says that if the wife is a better manager of money, then she should lovingly talk with her husband and suggest that she handle those areas. "She needs to speak up and not be a wimp, but say 'I do want to honor your perspective on things, but I want you to be aware of my needs.'" Even if the wife doesn't work outside the home, she should discuss her nonfinancial contributions to the household, such as preparing meals and caring for children. She shouldn't let shame at not earning an income keep her from being involved in decisions about money.

If you're uncomfortable approaching your husband about financial concerns, make a list of what you hope to improve in your household. Write down the most important points you need to discuss. Set up a time when the two of you can discuss your concerns without others being present. Sitting at the mall food court with children clamoring for attention is not the place to discuss serious family business. Neither is Thanksgiving dinner at your in-laws'.

Ask your husband what some of his concerns are about money and what he'd like to see change in your household. Try to avoid a lot of finger pointing and defensiveness, and remember you're working for the same team. Criticism should be constructive and not vindictive. Perhaps you're both engaging in harmful behaviors that need to be changed in order to heal your family finances, and you need to ask each other for forgiveness.

Maybe you're not married but have a roommate who isn't paying her fair share of the bills in your apartment. Take your list of concerns to this person and discuss them in an adult manner. Let her know that you want the living arrangement to work but that can only be accomplished by working together. If the situation has been dragging on for a long time with no solution and you're being threatened with eviction or other legal action because of a roommate's behavior, make plans to acquire separate residences as soon as possible. Don't stew in your anger and not take any action because you won't be "forced out." If the rent and utility bills are in your name and aren't paid, *your* credit report will suffer even if your roommate was supposed to help pay them.

The Root of the Problem

If you've been irresponsible with your finances, is it because deep down inside you feel you're owed something because you had a difficult childhood or other hardship in your life? Maybe constantly pressuring your mother to give you money or buy things for your children is a way of getting back at her for not providing the way she should have when you were young. Or maybe your parents gave you whatever you wanted as a child and you believe they should continue to do that, even though you're now forty and have your own family.

Perhaps you don't have any excuses for how you manage money, except that you just want to have a good time and not be bothered with serious issues. You may have children but are refusing to support them because you're angry that your ex-spouse got custody of them. But is it really fair for a parent to punish children in that way because their marriage relationship didn't work out?

Write down how you feel about your role in your financial situation. If you're still afraid or reluctant to admit any fault, why do you think that is? What do you think the consequences might be for confronting this issue? Are you feeling ashamed or embarrassed? Are you afraid others will find out that you don't have things together as much as they think? Will you be forced to behave differently toward other people in your life? Whatever you're feeling, tell yourself that it's more important for you to be happy with who you are as a person than to keep pretending everything is fine. Ask the Lord to help you be a more authentic person.

> ### Prayer Box
>
> *Lord, help me to look inside myself and have the courage to face my weaknesses. I ask that you would strengthen me to confront any negative behavior I may exhibit. I realize that blaming other people in my life for my financial problems will not change the situation. Help me make good choices as I continue to grow into financial maturity. Also give me courage to confront difficult situations with the people I love and care about in a way that will help us all to grow. Amen.*

Generational Legacies

Fathers, do not exasperate your children; instead, bring them up in the training and instruction of the Lord.

Ephesians 6:4

Sheila, 33, says she learned a lot about saving from watching her parents. As a child, she and her sister were given bank accounts one Christmas and taught how to read the statements and set aside a portion of their allowance. "My mom would sit with me and balance the account. Mom was very meticulous about keeping her bank statement and staying current," she says. "I used to be more meticulous but am now less diligent with it . . . and I think it's due more to laziness than anything."

Though she could save more, Sheila, an attorney, says she's still very frugal, a trait that's shared with her father. She remembers asking her father for money at times and getting the response that "he's not liquid," meaning he didn't have any cash to give her. "I think his frugalness really rubbed off on

> **Examine how your upbringing influences your current financial habits and beliefs. Decide what kind of financial legacy you want to leave.**

me. My husband and I are very cheap and try to make household items and things stretch."

By teaching her about saving and modeling responsible financial behavior, Sheila's parents created a positive generational legacy concerning money. But that kind of attention to teaching the next generation solid financial skills is absent in many families. For some kids, the only time they hear their parents discuss money is when they're arguing over the bills and how to get out of debt. That can leave a legacy with a child of believing that she, too, is destined to be in debt and will have a tough time managing money, says Dr. Anita Thomas of Northeastern Illinois University.

Other children never hear discussions about money. "Growing up, if I wanted something I would get it one way or another—although I was not born with a silver spoon in my mouth," says Melvita, 37. "But no one talked about money much. There was a lot of secretiveness about money." Melvita's experience is similar to that of many women interviewed for this book.

"It was feast or famine in our house. We would either have a lot of money or no money," says Rae, 55, about her parents' financial skills. "Sometimes we wouldn't have Christmas unless we had money." Because her father was an alcoholic and a gambler, Rae says her mother resorted to hiding money she earned so she could provide for the family. "There was no mention of money. You had it or didn't—there was no planning. It was something I had to learn on my own." Partly as a result of watching her parents' financial behavior, she says she developed a lot of poor habits herself.

Rae says it wasn't until many years later when she and her husband confronted their spending habits that they were able to come up with a plan to pay off a mountain of debt. "The debt was based on the life we had at that time. But now we are totally debt free, have no mortgages, and look at things a different way," she says. Tithing, changing her lifestyle, and making conservative investments in things such as real estate and bonds are keys to her current financial stability. This has allowed Rae to retire without feeling fearful over money and to devote much of her time to a women's ministry she helped start. "My focus is ministry oriented. My hope is different. My vision of the future is different."

Breaking the Cycle

What is your vision for the future? What kind of financial legacy would you like to pass on to the next generation? Do you even understand the financial legacy you've inherited from your parents or other adult role models?

Think about what patterns of behavior have consistently been a part of your system for handling money and other resources. Write these examples in your journal and indicate whether or not they're similar to behaviors exhibited by your parents. Also note whether these patterns are positive or negative.

Are you generally frugal because that's how you saw one or both of your parents behave? Do you constantly buy things on impulse? Is there a constant tug-of-war with your husband because one of you always wants to spend while the other values saving? Are you constantly buying things for your children as a way to appease your guilt for not having more time to spend with them? Are you consistent in your tithing and giving? You may be surprised by the number of similarities between your current financial behavior and that of your parents.

Now think about your beliefs concerning money and write them down. Make a note of whether or not you often heard any of these ideas from the adults around you as a child. For example, do you believe that no matter how hard you work, you'll never really get ahead financially and will always have to "work for the man"? Or are you confident that you'll be able to realize your dream of starting a small business, despite naysayers around you? Do you feel that it's inappropriate for parents to discuss financial issues in front of their children? Are you confident that you'll save enough for retirement with careful planning? Perhaps you feel you'll never truly be happy without a lot of money and possessions.

"There was a man all alone; he had neither son nor brother. There was no end to his toil, yet his eyes were not content with his wealth. 'For whom am I toiling,' he asked, 'and why am I depriving myself of enjoyment?' This too is meaningless—a miserable business!" (Eccles. 4:8). Like this man, who stopped to reflect upon why he was working so hard to gather wealth without any real satisfaction and no one to share it with, you should stop and think about your beliefs about money and how they influence your actions. Is this behavior advancing God's purpose for you? How do you think that behavior is being perceived by the next generation?

Role Models

Even if you don't have children of your own, your behavior is probably being observed by some of the young people who may be in your life. Think about it. Do you still remember certain adults you observed as a child who were always known for having the most fashionable wardrobes, expensive cars, or flashy jewelry? Did you and other kids dream about the day you could also have such extravagant things and be like Mrs. Fashionplate, who always came to church looking like she'd just stepped off a runway? Or maybe you wished for the day when you could have a fancy car like your neighbor, Mr. Cool, not realizing that he was up to his eyeballs in debt because of it.

If the financial behaviors modeled around you were positive, then hopefully they've rubbed off on you. But many adults neglect to teach their children about money while passing on harmful habits. "People do mirror what their parents do in every area—even finances," says Dr. Adriana Mueller, radio talk show host and a temperament therapist with Living Hope Ministry in West Orange, New Jersey. "Kids should see their parents be good stewards. But if there are bill collectors calling you and you're three months behind in the bills—and you're going out and buying a new television for your family—you're giving double messages."

Mueller says that people don't always realize they're modeling their parents' behavior. She uses the example of a wife who models her mother's behavior when she shops with her children, telling them to keep what she bought a secret from her husband. Not only is the woman setting herself up for marital conflict when her husband sees the receipts or credit card bills, but she's involving her children in a deception. In teaching their children to be good stewards, parents should refrain from showing deception to their children, Mueller says. "If there's something [wives] don't want their husbands to know, they should keep it to themselves and not bring the children into it."

But just because people may pick up bad habits from their parents doesn't mean they can't be broken. Once a person begins to understand the root of some of their financial habits and begins to focus on them, they can then work on making positive changes. Stop and think honestly about the generational legacy you may have received from your parents concerning your finances. If any of these issues are hindering your efforts to be a good steward, ask God to help you focus on changing them. Ask forgiveness for any disobedience to his Word, and pray for the courage to take any steps needed to conquer and move past them. "No, in all these things we are more than conquerors through him who loved us" (Rom. 8:37).

As you begin to confront any negative issues, refrain from blaming and accusing your parents or other relatives for their poor financial choices. Condemning others won't fix any problems you may have with your money and will only stir up unnecessary harshness and tension. The purpose of reflecting upon generational influences is to gain a deeper understanding of how you can become more responsible with your finances and honor God's Word.

Breaking Old Habits

You may find that you can no longer participate with family members in certain activities that are dependent upon poor financial decisions and behavior, such as chipping in for lottery tickets or taking spur-of-the-moment trips. Many families have started investing clubs, but if you really can't afford to belong because you have thousands of dollars in debt, explain to them that your financial future will look much brighter if you pay off this debt before seriously getting into investing. If you experience anger or pressure from family members, speak to them in a loving way and let them know that you are serious about getting your financial house in order and aren't judging them.

If you have children or know that you are an important influence in some child's life, pray about being a better example to young, impressionable minds. Don't be secretive about money. Talk openly about handling it responsibly and the importance of saving, especially if you give them an allowance. Write down some goals for talking to your kids about handling money responsibly. Look for good books that explain financial concepts at a level they'll be able to understand. Read Scriptures together that illustrate what God says about money and how it should be handled.

Traditionally, schools have done little to educate children about financial topics. A majority of students ages 16 to 22 have never taken a personal finance class and said they could use a few more money management lessons.[1] But that is changing as more schools launch financial literacy programs to teach children good money management skills, and legislators are calling for more education in this area. Churches are also getting more involved by offering financial ministries for adults and sometimes children.

But if you're a parent, the real responsibility lies with you for bringing up children who will be equipped with the knowledge, values, and integrity to be good managers of the resources they receive. Start a dialogue with them and be open about your family finances. Being secretive will only keep them in the dark and possibly contribute to them making poor decisions later on as adults. And while it's good for kids to learn from their mistakes, making an effort to begin educating them early on can help to avoid some of them.

> ### *Prayer Box*
>
> *Lord, thank you for helping me understand the generational legacies that may surround my financial habits. I don't want to blame others for my current actions, but I know that it's important to look at behaviors I may have inherited from my parents or other influential adults in my life. Please help me to be honest with myself about any negative habits I have and to be diligent about correcting them. Amen.*

Review Your
Monthly Bills

Do not forsake wisdom, and she will protect you; love her,
and she will watch over you.

Proverbs 4:6

was rushing to catch a train after a late meeting in New
York and decided to call my husband to let him know what
time to expect me home. Realizing that I'd forgotten my
cell phone that morning and didn't have enough change for
a pay phone, I reluctantly chose to call collect. Little did I
know that even though the call lasted less than a minute,
it would carry a very high price.

A couple weeks later when I received my regular phone bill,
my mouth fell open when I saw that I was being charged nearly
$12 for that call. While I expected to pay more than I would
have for a direct-dialed call, I couldn't believe that a phone
carrier could actually get away with charging such an exorbitant rate. After all, I hadn't called someone in Los Angeles; it
was a call from New York City to New Jersey, twenty miles

> **Read through bills to catch errors and guard against potential fraud. Create an orderly filing system for monthly bills and other important paperwork.**

away. The unfamiliar company's name next to the outrageous price prompted me to call my phone company for an explanation.

The customer service representative wasn't surprised when I said there had been no information at the pay phone or from the operator about what kind of rates would be charged. She explained that many pay phones are owned by independent companies that set their own rates, which can vary greatly. Sympathetic to my complaint, she promptly adjusted my account to delete the charge and warned me about using pay phones for such calls in the future.

This situation reinforced to me how important it is to closely examine monthly bills and other statements. While it may be more convenient to put these letters in a to-do pile for closer inspection later, reviewing them as soon as they arrive will quickly alert you to any errors or problems. It's amazing how many people don't bother to read the full content of their bills, but faithfully pay them each month.

Have you ever ignored the change-in-service notices that came in your cable or water bills and then wondered a couple months later why the fees rose but service remained the same? It's often the small service and maintenance fees that are increased unexpectedly, causing monthly payments to slowly creep upward. But changes in billing for existing services also occur. For example, the cost of two or more features on a phone line, such as voice mail and caller ID, averaged $12.35 in 2002, up 74 percent from 1999; the average monthly local phone bill rose to $38.25.[1]

The Bottom Line

Being a savvy consumer means understanding exactly where your money is going, so don't be afraid to call companies and ask questions about bills. "Blessed is the man who finds wisdom, the man who gains understanding, for she is more profitable than silver and yields better returns than gold" (Prov. 3:13–14).

New or unfamiliar charges on bills could also indicate fraud. According to the Federal Trade Commission, one of the biggest consumer complaints deals with "cramming," or unexplained charges on phone bills for services that were never ordered, authorized, or received. These charges generally are related to club memberships, such as travel clubs, and product or service programs, such as paging or calling cards. Other schemes include sweepstakes promotions that require dialing a toll-free number to claim a prize but turn out to be an automated line that enrolls the caller in a club or service program they don't necessarily want.

Pay attention to statements for services billed quarterly or even yearly, such as subscriptions, insurance premiums, trash removal, or home security. It's a good idea to keep the bill from the previous period in order to compare information. If there are fee increases or services you didn't request, contact the company for an explanation and ask whether they're mandatory.

Keeping good records and knowing what to toss out will help you better manage bills and other financial obligations. Even if you've never been very organized and generally "file" things into piles around the house, you can implement your own record-keeping system with little effort. Sort through any recent mail that may be stacked in to-do piles. Get in the habit of discarding junk mail as soon as you've looked through it to help cut down on clutter. If you don't have one, invest in a paper shredder to guard your privacy. Place banking statements and any bills that haven't been paid into a file folder or desk tray marked "Due This Month" so you can easily refer to them when making payments.

Pay all bills on time. If you're having money problems and don't have enough for all of your obligations, pay the essential debts and expenses first, such as food, necessary medical care, and housing. (Cable TV is not essential!) You may be able to get away with paying a minimum amount on basic utilities to avoid shut-off, or you may qualify for emergency assistance. If you need a car to keep your job, pay on that next and be sure to stay current on your auto insurance payments. Once a bill has been paid or you've used your bank statement to balance your checkbook, these items can then be filed using the following system.

Storing Records

Find a box or empty file drawer and designate that as the place where you will keep records. For very important documents such as car titles or deeds, you'll want to get a fireproof box or use a safe-deposit box. Purchase a package of file folders that you can label according to the type of papers you're filing.

Although only certain documents need to be kept for the long term, you're going to file all of your bills, financial statements, and other professional correspondence for a couple months until you've gotten used to reading through them and determining which ones need to be stored. Label the folders in a way that's easy for you to work with and place the paperwork in the appropriate one. Some people use letters of the alphabet and file things accordingly. I prefer to get even more specific and have folders labeled with specific bank account names, type of insurance, medical paperwork, credit card receipts, and so forth.

This task may seem simplistic at first. But even if *you* are an organized person who pays attention to these kinds of details, realize that there are many people out there who literally don't know where they put the telephone bill due *tomorrow*, the rent check, or even the checkbook. They may have so many piles of stuff lying around that the local fire inspector would probably issue a citation. Some of these folks may just be messy and disorganized, while others may be gripped with a hoarding attitude. And while some of them may tell you they know exactly where everything is, this really isn't the most efficient filing system or the best use of household space.

Monthly household and utility bills can generally be tossed after a couple of months, but should be kept longer in cases where they might be deductible on your tax return (i.e., if you use your basement for a home-based business). While you should keep bank statements for at least a year, there is no hard number for brokerage and other investment account records. Any records of transactions involving the purchase or sale of investments such as mutual funds should be kept so you can refer to them when filing tax forms. Copies of checks or other documents used to support tax returns should be stored with a copy of the return (see figure 5.1).

It may take a while to become accustomed to managing your paperwork on a consistent basis. Old habits can be hard to break, especially if you're used to just laying things anywhere around the house. But organizing records in this way will help you better manage your time, as well as clear out some of the clutter you may have in your home.

> ### *Prayer Box*
>
> *Lord, please help me to manage my time and resources better. I don't want to neglect bills and other important mail so that they pile up and create clutter. I want to be better organized and pay my financial obligations on time. I will take the time to carefully read through bills and other important paperwork and ask that you would give me the clarity to understand them and recognize any errors. Amen.*

Type of Document	How Long to Keep It	Where to Store It
Bank and brokerage statements; cancelled checks	At least one year, longer if expenses are deductible	Filing cabinet
Social security card; birth and marriage certificates; passport	Indefinitely	Fireproof box or safe-deposit box
Current insurance policies	Indefinitely (toss outdated policies)	Safe-deposit box or fireproof box
Stock and bond certificates	Indefinitely	Safe-deposit box (keep a list of these items in fireproof box)
ATM receipts	Until transaction is posted to statement	Filing cabinet
Tax returns	At least seven years	Filing cabinet
Mortgage paperwork	At least until paid off	Fireproof box
Loan paperwork	At least until paid off	Filing cabinet
Property deeds	Indefinitely	Safe-deposit box
Car titles	As long as you own the car	Safe-deposit box
Credit card statements	One year (longer if charges are deductible)	Filing cabinet

Type of Document	How Long to Keep It	Where to Store It
Wills and other estate planning documents	Indefinitely	File with attorney or keep in safe-deposit box (copy in fireproof box)
Service agreements and warranties	For the life of the contract	Filing cabinet
Receipts for large purchases/home improvements	Indefinitely	Filing cabinet or with home inventory
Documentation for expensive art and collectibles	Indefinitely	Safe-deposit box (copy with home inventory)
General household and utility bills	Two months (keep longer if they are deductible on tax returns)	Filing cabinet
Pay stubs	Through end of year until W-2 form or annual statement arrives	Filing cabinet

Figure 5.1

Your Credit Report

Every prudent man acts out of knowledge, but a fool exposes his folly.

Proverbs 13:16

Would you feel uncomfortable knowing that your coworkers were discussing your financial situation behind your back? Imagine that every time you step out of the room they begin buzzing about your salary, debts, or the value of your home. As more people join in the discussion, new and sometimes inaccurate information is exchanged. But these inaccuracies don't really matter to these people because they're just passing the time. Only by chance do you happen upon one of these conversations one morning. Stunned and embarrassed, you slink away quietly and don't even bother to stop the discussion or correct the mistakes.

This situation is similar to what happens with your credit report, which is an overview of your financial picture. Finance companies, insurers, and other institutions regularly review these reports to find customers to target with direct mailings and telemarketing. All those credit card offers, catalogs you didn't order, and solicitations from unfamiliar charities didn't end up in your mailbox by chance. The companies that sent them often have access to your name because they purchased a list of potential customers from a consumer reporting agency. Over 6 billion credit card offers were mailed to U.S. consumers in 2005, a 16% increase from 2004.[1]

> **Understand how information in your credit report is used. Get a copy of your report and check it for mistakes and outdated information. Remove your name from marketers' telephone and mail lists.**

These consumer reporting agencies—the most common being national credit bureaus such as Equifax, Experian, and TransUnion—are in the business of gathering and selling information on where you work and live, and whether you've been arrested, sued, or pay your bills on time. While this information is used by many companies strictly as a marketing tool, it's also used by employers, landlords, and other agencies to determine your creditworthiness and overall fiscal stability. Financial institutions routinely use these reports to calculate a credit score to help decide whether to extend credit or make a loan. The higher your score, the more favorably you're viewed.

Is this information trade legal? Yes. But that doesn't mean it's always completely accurate. And as frustrating as it may be to know that your personal information is being used in this manner, it's important to become educated about what is in your file. The Fair Credit Reporting Act (FCRA), which is enforced by the Federal Trade Commission (FTC), requires consumer reporting agencies to tell you everything in your report *if* you ask for it. At that time, these agencies also are required to give you a list of everyone who has requested your report in the past year, or in the past two years if the request was employment related.

Why let other individuals and organizations be privy to your personal information without you even knowing what they're seeing? Don't let fear or embarrassment keep you from obtaining your file and fixing any mistakes.

A Financial Report Card

If you've never seen a copy of your credit report, then you may have missed out on understanding some key information that might have affected the interest rate you received on a loan, your insurance premium, or that job you didn't get at a local bank. Credit reports can give information on whether you make child support payments, have a lien on your home, or filed for bankruptcy in the last ten years. They cannot give information on your race or religious affiliation. And contrary to a popular rumor spread via e-mail, not just anyone can have access to your information. Only people with legitimate business needs as recognized by the FCRA are entitled to see your report.

Contact at least one of the national consumer reporting agencies listed in figure 6.1 to request a copy of your report. Since the different agencies may not have the same information about you, it's a good idea to request your file from all three to check for any errors. Don't wait until a few days before making an offer for your dream house or applying for a small business loan to look at this information and then be blindsided by problems or mistakes. If you're planning a major purchase, request the report six months in advance if possible, so that you'll have time to fix any errors, pay down debt, or establish better bill-paying habits. Review your file about once a year, especially if you experience major life changes such as a divorce, or want to guard against fraud or identity theft. You can request one free copy from each of the three major credit-reporting bureaus every twelve months at www.AnnualCreditReport.com.

Major Credit Bureaus

Equifax	Experian	TransUnion
1-800-685-1111	1-888-397-3742	1-800-888-4213
www.equifax.com	www.experian.com	www.transunion.com

Figure 6.1

Depending on your reason for requesting the information, you may be eligible for a free report under FCRA guidelines. If you request the report within sixty days of receiving notice that your application for insurance, credit, or employment has been denied, you don't have to pay for it. Any letters you receive from companies denying you services or taking adverse action against you should have the name, address, and phone number of the consumer reporting agency they used. If you aren't eligible for a free report, you'll have to pay up to $9.50 for a copy, depending upon your state of residence. Figure 6.2 gives more information on when you're entitled to a free report.

You are entitled to a free credit report if:

1. You are a victim of fraud.
2. You request a report within 60 days of a company taking adverse action against you.
3. You are unemployed and plan to look for a job within 60 days.
4. You are on welfare.

Fair Credit Reporting Act

Figure 6.2

Once you receive your file, check it carefully for outdated information. In most cases negative information more than seven years old and bankruptcies older than ten years should not be included. If you find mistakes, write to the agency that issued the report and include copies of any evidence to support your claim. The agency must investigate your dispute by notifying the information source, and will correct or remove inaccurate or unverified items from your files, usually within thirty days.

Although seeing mistakes in your file and trying to clear them up can be frustrating, remember to stay calm and deal courteously with any agencies you have to contact, whether by letter or phone. The person handling your claim probably isn't personally responsible for the problem and is only trying to do their job. Even if they aren't very pleasant, avoid stooping to their level of behavior. If you do have difficulty keeping your temper in check or feel a lot of anxiety, try taking deep breaths and meditating on God's Word before making that phone call, and believe in his promise to provide for you. "Be still before the LORD and wait patiently for him; do not fret when men succeed in their ways, when they carry out their wicked schemes. Refrain from anger and turn from wrath; do not fret—it leads only to evil. For evil men will be cut off, but those who hope in the LORD will inherit the land" (Ps. 37:7–9).

Guarding Privacy

If it bothers you that your name and other personal information have become just another commodity to buy and sell, welcome to the club. Concerns about privacy have grown in recent years, partly because of the lucrative trade in consumer reports. Federal laws require banks, credit card companies, insurance companies, and brokerage firms to send mailings to customers each year explaining their policies on gathering consumer information. Financial firms that sell customer data to unaffiliated third parties must allow you to opt out of having your personal information sold. But if you don't read these policies and exercise your right to opt out of these lists, you'll probably continue to receive unwanted mail, phone calls, and e-mail. While it may be impossible to completely stop unwanted solicitations, there are steps you can take to curtail them.

The process of opting out has received a lot of attention, partly because so many privacy statements are extremely detailed and confusing. Somewhere in the mumbo jumbo they usually instruct you to call, mail in an attached form, or write your own letter to keep your name off mail and phone lists. (Never mind that you didn't ask to be placed on those lists in the first place!) But many of these notices don't address junk e-mails, commonly known as "spam," and you may still be required to log on to a web site to fill in another form for that.

If privacy is a concern to you, then make it a practice to read these notices and act on them as soon as they arrive. If you put them aside intending to go back to them later, they're likely to end up in the trash. To receive a privacy notice from a company with which you do business, call and ask for the form or just write them a letter stating that you are opting out of the sale of your personal information. But remember, there are tens of thousands of list compilers working from a variety of sources that may be difficult for you to constantly monitor. Anytime you subscribe to magazines and catalogs or buy products and services online, it's possible that your name will make its way onto a marketing list unless the company specifically states that it doesn't sell customer information or you ask them to keep it confidential.

Being listed in telephone directories, donating to charities, or entering sweepstakes are other sources for these lists. Major lifestyle changes often result in filings with government agencies, and records such as birth certificates, marriage licenses, and home sales are open to the public. Appendix B explains in more detail who some of these list compilers are, where they obtain their information, and how to contact them to remove your name from lists. If you want to know more about your rights under the FCRA or what you can do about unwanted mail or telemarketing, log on to the FTC web site at www.ftc.gov or call 1-877-FTC-HELP (1-877-382-4357).

Prayer Box

Lord, thank you for allowing me to have access to information that will help me better evaluate my financial situation. I don't want to be irresponsible with my money and want to take the necessary steps to solve any problems. If I find errors on my credit report, please help me to stay calm and rational when dealing with other individuals to fix them. I know this isn't a perfect world and that mistakes do happen. Amen.

DAY 7

Credit and Loans

The rich rule over the poor, and the borrower is servant
to the lender.

Proverbs 22:7

Ahhh, the first date. Looking, sounding, and smell-
ing good is a big priority, and often no expense is
spared. A man may spend days planning the perfect
outing just to impress a woman and convince her that he is
creative, romantic, and full of fun. A woman may splurge
by getting a new outfit and hairstyle. Both are usually on
their best behavior in an effort to let the other know what
a catch they are.

Most people out on a first date don't highlight any
downside or risk of getting involved with them. The possible long-term consequences of entering a relationship or
even marriage may be the furthest things from their mind,
and all too often outward appearances are the main focus.
But eventually the fun, romance, and awe of each other's good
looks tend to get upstaged by the realities of everyday life.

> **Establish a solid credit history without falling into the debt trap. Honestly evaluate your needs for loans and other credit, and shop around for the best deals.**

It's similar to finance companies saying "Pick me! Pick me!" by emphasizing the benefits of obtaining their loans or other services but not highlighting the years of tedious, costly, and even difficult obligations that may follow once a contract has been signed. And just as a couple that focuses mainly on outward appearances and superficial conversation while dating may have conflict if they later marry, a person who accepts a loan or credit card without fully investigating the terms may be in for a rude awakening.

The best rule to follow is to avoid loading up on credit cards and loans in the first place. Pay cash or write a check when making purchases, and don't buy what you can't afford. Using borrowed money makes it very easy to live above your means without even realizing it. "All man's efforts are for his mouth, yet his appetite is never satisfied" (Eccles. 6:7).

"When you eat more you get fat, and when you spend more you get in debt," says Rev. Patricia A. Davenport of Spirit and Truth Worship Center in Yeadon, Pennsylvania. Rev. Davenport says her church's financial workshops try to "help people get focused and stop keeping up with the Joneses. We don't even know where they live at, but supposedly they have a nice car and wear all these nice things."

The Pain of Debt

Decide if you are living above your means and what you hope to accomplish by doing so. Does having access to a high credit line make you feel important or more secure? Are you trying to make up for all the things you didn't have when you were growing up? Thomas Jefferson wrote in a letter to his daughter, Martha, dated June 14, 1787, "Be assured that it gives much more pain to the mind to be in debt, than to do without any article whatever which we may seem to want."[1]

Another alternative to the pain of debt is using a debit card to make purchases. These cards are accepted by many businesses and can be used like a credit card if they have a Visa or MasterCard logo. The money comes directly out of your bank account, so you can't spend what you don't have. But before using a debit card for purchases, make sure you understand any fees that might be involved. Also be careful about using cards linked directly to your bank account since credit card fraud and identity theft are on the rise, both on and off the Internet.

Because it's often difficult to obtain financial services or buy a home without a credit history, many people apply for a credit card as a means to establish one. This is fine, but only use this card if necessary and try to avoid carrying a balance each month. If you're recently divorced, separated, or widowed, and all of the credit cards and household accounts are in your husband's name, it's important for you to establish a credit history in *your* name. If you still live in the home you shared with your spouse, transfer the utilities and other services to your name ASAP and make it a point to pay for them on time. Cancel joint credit cards so you won't be liable for charges your ex-husband continues to make.

If you're going through a divorce, try to work out the financial arrangements as amicably as you can, especially if children are involved. But if things do turn ugly and you're worried about your credit rating being affected by your spouse's irresponsible behavior, consult your attorney to take steps to separate your financial obligations.

While it's important to establish a stable credit history whatever your marital status, you don't want to lose sleep at night because you're buried in debt. If you handle money responsibly, a credit card can be helpful in emergencies or when traveling. When you're tempted to spend by having that card in your wallet, keep it locked up at home until you absolutely need it. If you have no or poor credit history, you may be able to get a secured credit card requiring a cash deposit that matches a credit line of the same amount.

Before applying for a credit card or loan, really pray about whether it's absolutely necessary. Have you been laid off, depleted your savings, and feel you have no other alternative? Or perhaps you've been reluctant to cash in some of your investments to help pay debts. If you're employed and still struggling, did you consider moonlighting at a second job to supplement your income or selling belongings just gathering dust in your house? A loan isn't going to solve the underlying problems of what got you into trouble in the first place.

If you really believe you need a loan, remember that the banker in your community isn't trying to get your business just because he's a nice guy. Sure he may actually be a friendly, chatty person who coaches your kids at soccer, but the truth is that he and the bank he works for are looking to make money. And the more fees and interest you pay for the convenience of taking out that loan, the more that bank is going to profit. However, it's up to you, not the banker, to decide if you can really handle the costs of taking on a loan.

It's illegal to be denied a loan on the basis of your sex, race, or marital status, so if you feel a loan officer is asking inappropriate questions in these areas or exhibiting discriminatory behavior, you should move on to the next bank. You don't need that hassle, and many financial institutions have become savvy about the rising economic clout of women and are aggressively courting their business.

A Competitive Business

Many advertisements make obtaining loans sound like a breeze. All you have to do is call a toll-free number to apply and you'll receive an answer within a day or two, they promise. One TV commercial for a loan referral service even shows a banker hoping to score points with a couple who applied for a loan by bringing them breakfast in bed while other bankers haggle in their living room over giving them the best rate. The commercial implies that financial institutions are so eager to get a customer's business that they will do anything for them anytime.

Before applying, make sure you do your research and shop around for the best deal. Once the papers are signed, you'll be committed to handing over a portion of your paycheck each month to this debt. Check the current prime rate, which is the percentage rate at which banks will lend money to their most-favored customers, in the finance section of your local newspaper or the *Wall Street Journal*. The prime rate moves up or down based upon changes at the Federal Reserve Board. You can also check www.bankrate. com to see actual rates being charged by lenders around the country.

Find out the total amount, including fees and interest, to be paid back over the life of the loan. Knowing up front what to expect will keep you from being surprised later that the $2,500 you charged on your credit card, or the principal amount, turned into $4,000 because of only making minimum payments and being assessed late fees several times. The periodic rate mentioned in loan contracts refers to the interest rate the bank is charging to borrow money. But if there are other costs, such as annual or application fees, the annual percentage rate (APR), which is the actual rate of interest, will be higher. And the longer you take to pay off the balance, the more you pay because interest continues to accumulate.

Annual savings by switching to a credit card with a lower APR and no annual fee.

	Plan A	Plan B
Average monthly balance	$3,500	$3,500
APR	19%	14%
Annual finance charges	$665	$490
Annual fee	$25	$0
Total cost	$690	$490

Figure 7.1

In recent years more people have turned to so-called predatory lenders, which charge exorbitant fees to lend relatively small amounts of money. They include payday lenders, check cashiers, and rent-to-own stores, and are doing booming business with people who don't have checking accounts, can't get credit, and/or need money between pay periods. A payday lender will make a small loan based upon a personal check held for future deposit.

Let's say Gullible Gabby writes a personal check for $115. The lender agrees not to cash it until her next payday and gives her a $100 loan. If the lender charges a $15 fee for two weeks, that loan has an APR of 390 percent. In many states, if Gullible Gabby can't afford to pay the loan back, she can pay the $15 finance charge and roll over the remaining amount for a new total of $115. Now her finance charges total $30 for a $100 loan.[2] Avoid borrowing money from these places, which may encourage rolling over the loans so that they can continue to receive high interest.

If it's difficult to resist borrowing money, think about what is really causing you to take on more debt. Are you simply trying to establish a solid credit history? Or is it more important to get a prestigious-looking card that bears the name of the Ivy League school you attended? Are you waiting for the day when you can whip out a platinum card while dining with friends so they'll be impressed or jealous? Debt is debt. It doesn't matter whether it's run up on a gold, platinum, or polka-dotted card. You still have to pay it back.

The poet Paul Laurence Dunbar (1872–1906) summed up the financial as well as the psychological toll that can come with reckless spending:

> This is the debt I pay
> Just for one riotous day,
> Years of regret and grief,
> Sorrow without relief.
>
> Pay it I will to the end—
> Until the grave, my friend,
> Gives me true release—
> Gives me the clasp of peace.
>
> Slight was the thing I bought,
> Small was the debt I thought,
> Poor was the loan at best—
> God! but the interest![3]

When you pay off any loans you may have, it will become easier to be a lender instead of a borrower, as we're instructed in Deuteronomy 28:12—"The LORD will open the heavens, the storehouse of his bounty, to send rain on your land in season and to bless all the work of your hands. You will lend to many nations but will borrow from none." God wants us to have wealth and prosperity, but not at the expense of building his kingdom. Taking on multiple loans makes it difficult to get ahead with our own finances and to help others who may be in need of assistance.

Take a look at some of the web sites listed in appendix A to become better educated about loans and credit. Set aside paperwork for any credit cards or loans you want to refinance to get better rates. Day 8 will discuss finding better interest rates with your lenders.

Prayer Box

Father, help me to use credit wisely. Please strengthen my character so that I will make good decisions about living within my means and not becoming a slave to debt. I ask that you would give me the tools I need to carefully evaluate my options for borrowing and paying back money, and that you would give me favor with any lenders or financial institutions with which I do business. Amen.

Get Rid of Debt

Let no debt remain outstanding, except the continuing debt to love one another, for he who loves his fellowman has fulfilled the law.

Romans 13:8

A twenty-something Brooklyn woman named Karyn came up with an unusual way to pay off over $20,000 of debt. Setting up a web site, she put out an appeal to anyone who cared to send her at least a dollar to put toward her bill. The woman, who didn't reveal her last name or show her face on the web site, explained that frivolous spending on such things as designer clothes, beauty salon visits, and other pricey purchases had taken a toll. She also claimed to be reformed from her poor spending habits.

While this sounds pretty ridiculous and you're probably wondering who would send money to a stranger who won't show her face, the fact is that within about four months, Karyn paid off the total debt with about $13,000 received through her web site. She paid the remainder of her debt out

> **Take responsibility for how your behavior may have contributed to debt and other money problems. Form a debt reduction strategy and evaluate the benefits of refinancing or consolidating loans.**

of her paychecks and from money earned selling goods on the auction web site eBay.[1]

Not surprisingly, after news got out about Karyn's experience, a slew of similar "cyberbegging" web sites began popping up with emotional appeals for money for such things as paying medical bills, buying a car, and helping a woman divorce her husband. But setting up such money-raising schemes doesn't reflect taking responsibility for one's own actions or financial maturity. By looking for a quick fix these people may have overlooked the root of their money problems.

Have you been looking for a quick fix and dodging your responsibilities? Are your debts and other obligations piled up like mountains of smelly garbage during a sanitation strike? Maybe you don't see anything wrong with getting other people to pay your debts, and regularly coax others into giving you money. Perhaps it's not completely your fault that you're in a financial bind, because you were laid off from your job and still need to feed your kids. Maybe your husband left you and you're at a loss about what to do. Whatever your situation, there is hope for sorting through the mess and knocking down that debt.

Going through your credit card statements and other bills may have been a relatively painless experience, or it may have raised your anxiety level a couple notches by re-emphasizing how much money you owe. But before you have a panic attack, stop and ask God to help you stay calm and focused on implementing a plan to correct this area. Ask his forgiveness if you've been looking for others to blame for your situation or felt you were entitled to handouts to solve your problems. While I want to emphasize that there's nothing wrong with helping those who legitimately need it, it's important that individuals learn to cope with their own issues and develop problem-solving skills.

Avoiding Responsibility

For many people, dealing with debt involves more cunning than displayed by the Artful Dodger, the little pickpocket in the Charles Dickens novel *Oliver Twist,* who was particularly good at—and proud of—his vice. But the Dodger, like the other children in that tale, was being led and influenced by the adults in his life. If you're a parent, anytime you ask your children to say that "Mommy and Daddy aren't home" when creditors call and you just don't want to be bothered, aren't you being an artful dodger as well as training your kids to assume that role later? And if you actually have no intention of paying your debts, your children may eventually figure that out and see your dishonesty.

Do you want children to grow up seeing you handle your finances dishonestly and immaturely, or do you want them to model themselves after your godly decision to take responsibility for your situation and acknowledge your mistakes? "LORD, who may dwell in your sanctuary? Who may live on your holy hill? He whose walk is blameless and who does what is righteous, who speaks the truth from his heart" (Ps. 15:1–2).

You may be thinking, "But I just told a little white lie," or "I'll take care of it later. What's the harm?" Well, those tactics don't harm creditors, but they can make your situation even worse. Besides hurting your credibility and your credit rating, you may be hit with high interest rates and penalty fees for not making payments. Another consequence of dodging your bills is that your wages may be garnished, which means a court may order your employer to pay a percentage of your salary directly to people you owe.

Lenders may also sell any property you've put up as collateral, or liens may be attached to your home. If a creditor feels they've exhausted all attempts to get the money, the amount may be completely written off as an uncollected debt and show up on your credit report for seven years. If your debts become too unmanageable, you may be forced into bankruptcy. All of the above actions can harm your chances of getting a mortgage or getting hired for certain jobs.

If you've been acting like an artful dodger, maybe it's because you really don't know how to get out of the mess you're in or where you're going to find the money to pay back the people you owe. Maybe you're like one woman I spoke with who, when asked what she thinks it will take to get rid of thousands of dollars of debt, replied, "I think it would take a big loan!" Or perhaps you've spent so much time running from problems that you aren't sure where to begin correcting them. Maybe you've been relying so much on *you* that you haven't taken time to ask the Lord for *his* help. Ask him to be your rock and shield and to guide you while making plans to pay off debt.

If It's Broke, Fix It

Instead of avoiding your creditors the next time they call, speak with them calmly and let them know that you intend to honor your debts and want to work out a payment plan. Although there are some unscrupulous people working in the collection industry, often the folks you're dealing with are more than willing to negotiate a plan that's satisfactory to all parties involved. You can even ask if they're willing to rewrite your loans to adjust the payment amount and extend the length of time you have to pay. Be aware that doing this will raise your total cost since the creditor will charge you interest for a longer period of time.

If you're having trouble repaying student loans, you may be able to set up a new plan that lowers your payments or get a deferment, which postpones them for a specific period of time. If you're having temporary financial difficulty, you may be eligible for a forbearance, which allows payments to be suspended or reduced for a period of time. During that time, interest will continue to accrue and be added to the principal balance at the end of the forbearance period.

Cut up credit cards if you can't stop using them. Then review your statements and shop around for better interest rates. If you find one and your current credit card company won't match it, tell them you plan to transfer the balance to the other card. If you find an offer for a lower fixed interest rate until the transferred balance is completely paid off, sign up and pay your bill on time each month. Don't miss any payments or your interest rate will probably be increased.

Always read the fine print on credit offers so that you understand what the APR on the account is. If there are special introductory rates for several months, the fine print will say what the interest will be after that period ends. After the balance has been transferred and you've received a statement from the new finance institution confirming that, write a letter to close out the old account and destroy the card—even if you requested over the phone that the account be closed.

Once you've gotten better interest rates, choose the account with the highest interest rate to pay off first and put as much extra money as you can spare toward those payments while continuing to pay other debts. Once you've paid off that account, roll over the monthly payment into another one of your debts until it is paid off. Continue rolling over payments until you're free and clear of all debts. Be sure to write to finance companies to close any lines of credit that have been paid off.

Many people turn to loan consolidators to pay debts. These private companies lend money to combine debts into one monthly payment. Usually you get lower monthly payments for a longer period of time, but you may end up paying high interest rates and fees. Ads run on television, radio, and in newspapers every day offering consolidation and credit counseling services, sometimes for ridiculously high monthly fees. If you feel that you really need outside help, a nonprofit credit counselor that offers free consultations or charges a relatively small fee is probably the best route. Many churches are also becoming involved with providing financial counseling and education at no charge, so if you have access to this take advantage of it. You don't have to pay someone to get out of debt if you take time to set up a workable plan and stick with it.

The worst-case scenario to solving debt problems is filing bankruptcy and should be avoided at all costs. Over 2 million Americans filed for personal bankruptcy protection in 2005, according to the American Bankruptcy Institute. Many of these people rushed to avoid changes in the federal bankruptcy law that took affect later that year, making it more difficult to file. One of these changes requires mandatory credit counseling before a bankruptcy filing can be made. With total consumer debt more than

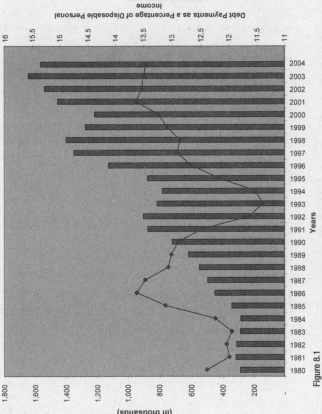

Influence of Total Consumer Debt on Bankruptcy Filings
Trends by Year 1980-2004

Figure 8.1

$2.15 trillion, it's no wonder so many people are in over their heads.[2] However, keep in mind that filing bankruptcy will hurt your credit rating. What it won't do is solve poor money management skills, compulsive spending, or other issues in your life (see figure 8.1 on p. 75).

If you really feel bankruptcy is your only option, consult an attorney to make sure you understand exactly what's involved and what your legal rights are. If you file Chapter 7 bankruptcy, you'll sell all your assets (with the exception of those that are exempt) to pay creditors and ask to be freed of debts. Chapter 13 bankruptcy allows you to keep your home and work out a payment plan with creditors. A trustee will oversee this plan, which stretches for three to five years.

Even if your efforts to pay down mountains of debt don't seem to be moving fast enough, don't be discouraged. If it took years for your finances to get in their present state, why expect to change everything in just a few months? If you stay focused and faithfully work to change your habits and be disciplined, you'll see progress.

Prayer Box

Lord, thank you for putting the spirit of discipline in me. I don't want to be in bondage to debt and am willing to work hard at not living above my means. I am so glad that you've equipped me with the tools to change my situation and establish good habits. I know that I don't have to spend money to be happy. I continue to rely on you to uplift and strengthen me as I continue on with my financial makeover. Amen.

Know Your Savings

Wealth and honor come from you; you are the ruler of all things. In your hands are strength and power to exalt and give strength to all.

1 Chronicles 29:12

Women in the U.S. are earning more money than ever, and many are reaping the benefits of financial independence. While they are taking a more active role in managing their household finances than a decade ago, their view of money often differs from that of men. Women, who are trained as nurturers, tend to view money as a means to create a lifestyle and spend it on things that enhance daily living. Men, who are trained to fix and provide, tend to see money as something to be captured and accumulated.[1]

"I'm waiting to be able to stop working a while to be home more with my son, but not being able to afford it," says Lorine, 39, who works for a bank. "If I really wanted or needed to would I be able to quit?" Overall, Lorine says she's

> **Decide that saving is a priority and make good decisions that support this goal. Gather statements for savings accounts and add them up to get a total.**

comfortable with her family's financial situation and has no real apprehension about their ability to maintain their current standard of living or meet future goals. She feels that faithful tithing and giving, as well as careful money management, have blessed her at home as well as professionally.

But Lorine is interested in starting a savings plan for her son's college education, which begins in about six years. She and her husband are hoping their son will get scholarships or take advantage of the full-tuition scholarship at the state university for students who maintain a B average. Still, Lorine knows that with educational costs continuing to rise there really isn't much time and that putting more effort toward planning in this area will ultimately benefit her family.

"I've always been more of a saver," she says. "And I always think we can save more." To meet savings goals, Lorine plans to increase the frequency of her monthly meetings with her husband to discuss major financial decisions, and she feels that prayer will continue to bring them into agreement. "But the biggest part for us is seeking God's will for us," she says.

Financial Gains

Lorine is wise to plan ahead and is among the growing number of women who are taking a more active role in their family finances. About 30 percent of married or cohabiting women in 2002 with household incomes of $50,000 or more had sole responsibility for saving or investing for retirement, while 61 percent shared that duty with a spouse or significant other.[2] But though women are making financial gains overall, only 14 percent had $100,000 or more saved for retirement, compared with 21 percent of men.[3] That's despite the fact that women have longer average life spans than men.

Think about what steps you've taken to plan for the future. Has saving money been a priority in your life, or do you spend more than you can keep? Is your desire to build a nest egg being derailed by frequent shopping binges and other compulsive spending habits?

Perhaps it's been difficult to build a savings because you've experienced emergency situations such as an illness, a job loss, or a leaky roof that depleted what you managed to put aside. Or maybe you just didn't anticipate how long it would take to save for a large purchase and are now short of cash. Whether you're trying to save enough to buy a new car, provide piano lessons for your child, or take a trip to Europe, it's important to have a clear goal and follow through with it. "He who ignores discipline comes to poverty and shame, but whoever heeds correction is honored" (Prov. 13:18).

Poor planning and bad decisions can wreak havoc on a savings plan. "I make decently wise decisions with money overall, but it seems to me that periodically I make one bad decision that costs me a pretty penny," says Sharon, a forty-something educator and divorced mother of two. She says her money troubles tend to revolve around her car, such as when it got towed and she had to pay about $1,000 for parking tickets and other penalties. "That was more of a lack of wisdom that cost my finances."

Sharon's poor decision making about her car also has resulted in breaking down on the highway because she didn't do regular vehicle maintenance and having to pay over $6,800 at the end of a three-year lease because of a clause relating to damages. She says most of the damages were basic wear and tear to the car but admits she should have paid more attention to the contract. "If I had inquired more of the Lord . . . then I wouldn't have had those problems," Sharon says. "I should be listening and obeying and doing more things myself."

Making Wiser Choices

Think about some of your decisions that may have hindered efforts to save. Be prepared to accept your role in areas that may have blocked your growth. If poor planning or some other problem needs to be addressed, then write a goal statement for overcoming that weakness. Perhaps your goal is to take more time deciding how to allocate funds, or to stop being in denial about squandering money that could be saved.

Many people open Christmas club accounts at their bank and make occasional deposits throughout the year so they'll have enough to shop with during the holidays. This is a good strategy for short-term savings goals and doesn't have to be limited to Christmas accounts. But for long-term planning, establish fixed automatic deductions from each paycheck to go into an account. You can also write a check to deposit, but with automatic deductions you won't be as tempted to spend the money.

Look through any statements for savings you currently have such as money market accounts, certificates of deposit (CDs), or savings bonds. Which accounts are liquid, meaning if you needed the money tomorrow you'd be able to get it without paying penalties? CDs and savings bonds generally require you to deposit money for a specific period of time in order to earn interest, so that money isn't easily accessible. Cash kept in a passbook savings account is.

Total up your savings; include any cash you may keep in a vault or safe-deposit box. You will refer to this information again during your 25-day makeover. Don't feel discouraged if you don't have any savings. The next chapter will help solidify your goals and determine which savings tools are best for your situation.

Prayer Box

Lord, I want to be a more disciplined saver. I know that I can make better use of my resources and not squander what I've been given. Help me to prioritize my savings goals and put steps in place to accomplish them. Please touch me in a fresh way so that I will make good decisions on a consistent basis. Amen.

DAY 10

Savings Goals

The LORD sends poverty and wealth; he humbles and he exalts.

1 Samuel 2:7

f you lost your job tomorrow, would you be able to meet your financial obligations for the next three to six months? Are you even aware of how much you'd need to live on for that period of time? If you do have a savings fund that would cover such an emergency, then you're steps ahead of many Americans. In 2001, 59 percent of all U.S. households were reported to have accumulated some savings.[1] That means the rest of those households haven't managed to save anything despite increasing income levels.

Take a look at the amount calculated in the last chapter for your total savings. Is it enough to cover the rent or mortgage for a few months? Think about all the other obligations besides housing that need to be met. If you've been keeping track of your spending, you can refer to some of those amounts to determine how much money needs to be saved to cover several months of expenses. Otherwise, add up the total for three months of your household income and use that as a rough estimate for an emergency savings. If you feel that you need a bigger cushion, total up the amount for four to six months, depending on your situation. These emergency funds should be kept in a savings account that you can access easily.

> **Evaluate the types of savings accounts offered at financial institutions by comparing rates, services, and other information. Form savings goals and build up emergency funds.**

When deciding on what type of account to open, first look at how much interest you'll earn, or the percentage of the deposit the financial institution pays for being allowed to use your money. The more often interest is paid, the higher the yield will be because it is being calculated using the new amount each time, increasing the return on your money.

Types of Accounts

Statement savings accounts are probably what most people think of when beginning a savings plan. The advantages of these accounts are that they are accessible on short notice, have low or no balance requirements, and are insured for up to $100,000 by the Federal Deposit Insurance Corporation (FDIC). One drawback, however, is that they tend to pay low interest, so you won't get much of a return on your money. A statement is sent out by the bank with the account balance. A passbook savings account is basically the same, except that each time a deposit or withdrawal is made the account holder's passbook is stamped and there are no statements mailed out.

Credit unions are an alternative to traditional banks. These nonprofit institutions are run by the people they serve, such as employees at the same company. Accounts generally have low fees and are often insured by the FDIC. Credit unions appeal to many people because the requirements for joining and for obtaining loans often aren't as strict as at other financial institutions. Another advantage is that many companies allow employees to have money deposited directly from their paychecks into credit union accounts to build a savings or to pay back loans. The downside is they often have very low interest rates on savings and very few ATMs.

Bonds are debt securities where the money invested is lent to the corporation or government that issued the bond in exchange for a fixed interest rate. That interest is paid either at specific times over the life of the bond or when it matures. The principal is repaid when the bond matures. Savings bonds are issued by the U.S. Treasury Department and their earnings are exempt from state and local income taxes. Federal taxes can be deferred until the bonds reach final maturity or until they're redeemed. Savings bonds can be bought for as little as $25, but may be purchased in smaller increments with the Payroll Savings or EasySaver plans that allow automatic purchases from checking and savings accounts. You can't redeem the money until six months after the bond is issued and will pay an early redemption penalty if it's been less than five years.

Money market funds are mutual funds that invest in high-quality, short-term government and corporate debt securities. They earn a variable interest rate and the money can be withdrawn at any time without penalties. While money in these accounts is not FDIC insured, they are considered a relatively safe investment.

Money market accounts are interest earning savings accounts that usually pay more interest than regular savings accounts but usually require a minimum balance. They also have restrictions on the number of withdrawals that can be made without additional fees being assessed. These accounts are insured by the FDIC and differ from money market funds, which are not.

To earn more of a return on savings, many people turn to certificates of deposit (CDs), which have a fixed length of time for the deposit ranging from three months to five years. Although CD interest rates have fallen from highs of over 15 percent in the 1980s, they still generally have a higher rate of return than basic savings accounts. They're also insured up to $100,000 by the FDIC. But because penalties are charged for early withdrawals, these accounts are best for money that doesn't have to be accessed on short notice.

Compare Levels of Service

When you're ready to open an account, shop around and compare different financial institutions. Ask for brochures that explain the different types of accounts, services, and fees. Are you looking for a big bank that has a large presence in your area or a smaller one with more personalized service? If you think you'll want additional services beyond checking and savings, ask for information on what's being offered.

Also, think about when and where you usually do your banking. Do you need a bank branch or ATM near your job? Is it safe to use the ATM after banking hours? Are ATMs owned by the bank regularly stocked with enough envelopes and supplies?

Now that you have some idea of the types of accounts available, think about your personal needs. If you don't have an emergency fund, then that should be your first savings priority. But if you carry a lot of credit card debt and must decide between paying it off and building a savings, it makes more sense to pay off the debt first. That's because the interest charged on credit cards is usually much higher than what you'd earn on a savings account.

Once you've built up an emergency reserve, you can get more aggressive about planning for specific goals and save at least 10 percent of your income. Are you planning for a major life event such as purchasing a house, staying home with your newborn for several months, or sending your kids to college? Maybe you intend to pay cash for a new car or renovate your kitchen. Write down a list of short-term versus long-term savings goals and an estimate of how much money you will need for each of them. Short-term goals are anything that will require access to cash within a year or two and may or may not be flexible depending on your situation.

Look at your list and prioritize your goals. If you've recently paid off old debts, use the money that would have gone toward them to build your savings. Decide how much of that money should go toward a specific short-term goal such as saving for a new water heater, as opposed to a more general fund for long-term plans. Maybe you'll have to postpone saving for a vacation because it's more important to pay for your son's braces.

If you aren't used to saving it may take some time to build the discipline to keep stashing money instead of spending it. Use the automatic deductions method if you know that you won't make deposits yourself. As time passes, you'll be pleased at how these deposits add up without your doing any work other than checking your account statements to make sure they are accurate and continue to reflect the best interest rates you can get.

Prayer Box

Lord, thank you for giving me the tools to start and follow through with a savings plan. You have provided so much for me and I want to handle these resources in a way that pleases you. I understand that building a savings will require effort on my part and less focus on spending. I don't want to become a hoarder, but I know that it is important to set aside money for future goals. Amen.

Planning
for Retirement

He died at a good old age, having enjoyed long life, wealth and honor. His son Solomon succeeded him as king.

1 Chronicles 29:28

Anne*, 53, had always looked forward to retirement and having more leisure time to pursue some of her hobbies. She and two friends had talked for years of traveling together after retiring and had already chosen some of the exotic locales they planned to visit. She'd gotten a late start with saving for retirement because she didn't have to work outside of the home until she and her husband divorced after ten years of marriage and she was left to raise two children on her own. The first couple of years were rough, but things improved financially after she found a job as an administrative assistant to a high-level executive.

Eventually, Anne saved enough to buy a modest town house and began having a portion of each paycheck deposited into a 401(k) retirement account. She didn't save much

*Anne is a composite of several women.

outside of this retirement plan, but following the suggestions of an advisor at the investment company that handled her account, she kept the bulk of her money in several high-risk mutual funds that had large gains during much of the 1990s. Confident that the stock market would continue to soar and she'd have enough money for retirement, Anne paid little attention to the 401(k) and relied heavily on the broker to make decisions. She didn't really understand how the stock market worked anyway and always seemed to be busy with other tasks.

> **Look at your expectations for retirement and write a goal statement. Understand the role of social security in retirement. Calculate how much you've saved for retirement.**

Now Anne is alarmed at how much money her 401(k) has lost over the past couple years as the economy has struggled. After several years of stellar gains, Anne's retirement account lost 50 percent of its value in just two years, as if somebody let half of the air out of some little kid's balloon. Her broker has told her that she should have been more diversified, but she isn't even sure she understands what that means or why he didn't tell her that before. "Maybe I should have paid more attention to those quarterly statements or put more aside," she says, shaking her head sadly. But one thing she does understand: the early retirement that she'd planned to take in a few years will have to be postponed indefinitely as she continues to work and save up more money.

Sinking Retirement Funds

Anne's case isn't unique. At the end of 2002, about 25 percent of Americans between the ages of fifty and seventy who owned stocks had lost 25 percent to 50 percent of their investments since the economy stalled in 2000. As a result of the losses, 21 percent of those people said they had postponed retirement, and 12 percent of those who weren't working or seeking work at the time of the poll said they might have to look for a job in the future.[1]

Perhaps you're among this group of people who've been blindsided by dramatic losses in a retirement fund. Maybe you still have quite a few years left until retirement but are appalled at how your account has dwindled away. If you don't have any retirement funds saved, you may be wondering what all the fuss is about. You probably haven't put any effort toward planning for the future because it's too far away and you believe you'll get by with social security or ... well ... something. But hoping to "get by" isn't the way to plan for much of anything, let alone such an important season of life as retirement.

When it comes to planning for retirement, Americans fall into five distinct groups, according to the 2002 Retirement Confidence Survey of one thousand individuals twenty-five and older. Planners, or 23 percent of Americans, are disciplined savers and financial risk takers who believe anyone can retire comfortably with planning. Savers, 19 percent, are careful with money and seldom experience setbacks due to unexpected events, but tend not to be investors. Strugglers, 18 percent, frequently suffer financial setbacks, although many consider themselves to be disciplined savers. Impulsives, 24 percent, feel that a comfortable retirement is possible, but are prone to impulse buying and financial setbacks. Deniers, 15 percent, dislike financial planning and rarely plan ahead.[2] Which category do you think you fall into? (See figure 11.1.)

Statements Describing Financial Attitudes

Statement Describes Respondent:

	Very Well	Well	Not Too Well	Not At All
Just when I think I have a handle on my finances, something always happens that sets me back from my financial goals.	27%	24%	31%	18%
I am disciplined at saving.	25%	39%	27%	9%
Over the long run—ten to twenty years—I believe stocks in general will be a very good investment.	22%	34%	20%	19%
I am not willing to take any financial risks, no matter what the gain.	20%	21%	34%	25%
I enjoy financial planning.	21%	37%	25%	16%
I frequently spend money when I do not plan to buy anything.	10%	19%	37%	33%

The 2002 Retirement Confidence Survey, Employee Benefit Research Institute, American Savings Education Council, Mathew Greenwald & Associates, Inc.

Figure 11.1

Write down a list of goals for your retirement years. This may be the first time you've really thought about what you'd like to do when you reach that point. If you have a difficult time envisioning a future where you no longer have to work, perhaps that's because you don't have your financial house in order and struggle every day to make ends meet. Or maybe a large part of your identity is tied up in your occupation and you haven't cultivated much of a personal life.

Take a few moments to imagine your ideal scenario and what that will mean to you financially. Do you dream of traveling like Anne, or will you be content to stay close to home and perhaps get more involved in your community? Maybe you want to mentor youth in your church or take classes at a local college. Write down how much money you think you'll need to retire comfortably and accomplish these goals. Give it your best guess. Later you'll actually calculate a more accurate amount and compare the two to see if you were close.

Visualizing the Future

Think about how confident you feel about the future. Does it make you nervous or even afraid to visualize it? Sometimes people say they believe God will provide for their needs but then allow themselves to be consumed with fear and apprehension about what will happen from one moment to the next. Read Matthew 6:25–34 and reflect upon how God has provided and will continue to provide for you. Make notes in your journal if that helps.

About 70 percent of workers twenty-five and older who were polled in 2002 said they were very or somewhat confident of having enough money to live comfortably throughout their retirement years, and 10 percent said they weren't at all confident. At the same time, only a third of all those polled said they had tried to calculate how much money they'll actually need to live comfortably.[3] High net worth members of Generation X (Americans born between 1966 and 1975) said they believe they'll need $2 million to retire, even though most aren't anywhere on track to saving that much.[4]

Whether you think you'll need $2 million or some other amount to retire comfortably, it's your job to begin saving for that. Don't just ask the Lord to enlarge your territory and then sit back and do nothing. Ask him for what you need, be obedient to his will, and really believe those requests will be honored. He's given you the tools you need to plan ahead for your retirement and it's up to you to use them. "For the LORD is good and his love endures forever; his faithfulness continues through all generations" (Ps. 100:5).

Because women are more likely to live longer than men, they can't afford not to plan ahead. A woman who is now 65 can expect to live to 85, while a 65-year-old man can expect to live to 81. So even if a woman is married, there is a greater chance of her outliving her husband and having to provide for herself than vice versa. Women also tend to earn less than men and move in and out of the workforce more often because of child-rearing issues. As a result, they often have fewer financial resources in retirement. Of the 59 million employed women in the U.S. as of June 2000, only 47 percent participated in a pension plan.[5]

Many people who don't plan ahead may be relying solely on receiving social security payments to fund their retirement years. While there's much debate about whether or not social security will even be available to future generations, the fact remains that most people require more than those monthly payments to maintain a standard of living similar to that during their working years. Also, not only do social security payouts depend on a person's earnings over their lifetime and the age at which they retire, but they may differ in situations where people are disabled, widowed, or caring for children. The average retiree receives about 40 percent of their pre-retirement earnings from social security.[6]

To find out how much social security income you can expect to receive during retirement, contact the Social Security Administration and ask for a Social Security Statement that details estimated benefits based on your earning history and when you would be eligible to receive them. If you're married you should ask for statements for both spouses. You can request your free statement at 1-800-772-1213 (www.ssa.gov).

If you've already begun saving, you'll need to determine exactly how much you've put aside so far. Gather the most recent statements for any retirement accounts you already have. If your employer has a pension program, find any paperwork that explains how it works. You'll use this information later to calculate how much money you need to save for your retirement needs. Although it may be tempting to ignore retirement planning if you still have twenty or more years until retirement, don't be fooled into thinking it's not important and should be put off until later. The earlier you begin saving, the better off you'll be.

Prayer Box

Dear Lord, thank you for providing for my needs. Help me to be faithful in handling my finances and give me wisdom when planning for the future. I will not let fear hinder my actions and keep me from making sound decisions. Help me to have a vision for my future and understand how retirement will be a part of it. I know that the decisions I make today will influence what happens later. Amen.

Retirement Income

> He who gathers crops in summer is a wise son, but he who sleeps during harvest is a disgraceful son.
>
> Proverbs 10:5

Retirement isn't cheap. Not only is the average life span longer, but older people are more active and in better health than in previous generations, making it conceivable that many people will spend up to twenty-five or thirty years in retirement. But how much money is enough to live on?

Generally, financial experts say that the average person will need to replace at least 70 percent of their pre-retirement income in order to maintain the same standard of living they had during their working years. So if you currently earn $60,000 a year, you'll need at least $42,000 a year in retirement income to have the same standard of living. Multiply that by the number of years you expect to live in retirement for a total amount. For example, a person who needs $42,000 a year and expects to spend twenty-five years in retirement

Calculate how much money you need to retire comfortably. Evaluate different retirement plans. Sign up for employee-sponsored and other retirement plans.

will need about $1.05 million. Using your current annual income and the number of years you estimate you'll live in retirement, figure out how much you'll need.

How does your calculation compare with your estimate from the previous day? If you're living paycheck to paycheck and having trouble meeting your monthly financial obligations, this may seem like a pretty intimidating amount. But if you're serious about saving and making your money work better for you by getting good returns, then it's time to refocus your priorities.

How much you need to save for retirement will also be influenced by your potential housing costs, any plans to work after retiring, and other large expenses. Many people scale back during retirement years and move from a larger, more expensive home to one requiring less money and upkeep. If you plan to have your mortgage paid off before retiring, that's one large expense you won't have to worry about. But if you have children who will be in college around the same time you retire, then educational costs may be an important part of planning ahead.

Sources of Income

Now look at what specific sources of income you can expect to have for retirement. List the amount estimated on your social security benefits statement. Then examine the statements for any retirement plans you already own. Write down the type of account, total, and what kind of securities it may be invested in. If you know the rate of return on the account also include this. Check your quarterly or annual statements to see if they include this information. Ideally, you'll want funds invested in retirement accounts to earn interest of 7 percent to 8 percent a year.

Write down whether or not the account is an employee-sponsored retirement plan. If you're not sure whether or not your employer has a pension or other retirement plan, talk with the employee benefits department to review your situation. Many companies don't offer pension plans where the company pays out retirement benefits without worker contributions, so it's important to know whether or not this is the case. If your company has a retirement plan that you aren't participating in, sign up and work toward contributing the maximum that's allowed. Not only do many employers contribute to such plans, but they're usually tax-deferred, meaning that you don't pay taxes on money contributed until it's withdrawn at retirement.

Total up the amount of your anticipated retirement income from all sources. If you're married, add up any expected income from your spouse. Are you on track to having enough to live on later in life? Do you need to save more aggressively in order to have enough funds? If you're still finding it difficult to believe you'll be able to save enough, close your eyes and visualize yourself as a prosperous person. Does your vision include being a faithful steward, making wise financial decisions, and being rewarded with God's resources throughout your entire life? See yourself as God wants you to be, exceedingly and abundantly blessed.

Also consider whether you have other assets such as a home or business that you plan to sell later. If so, add the value of these assets to your total to determine how much income you'll have for retirement. If you have a financial software program on your computer, use any retirement planning tools there to keep track of your progress saving. If you don't have a retirement account or are looking to diversify your funds, the next section gives an overview of some of the more common pension and retirement plans.

Choosing a Plan

Defined-benefit plans are funded by employers and usually don't require employee contributions. Benefits are given as a lump sum or guaranteed monthly payments, and the amount the employee is eligible for is usually based on their salary and years at the company. These plans are becoming less common as many companies put more of the burden of saving for retirement on employees. The number of private-sector workers who had traditional pensions fell to 23 million in 2002 from 29 million in 1985.[1]

Defined-contribution plans require employees to contribute and may or may not include contributions from the employer. Benefits are paid out as a lump sum or in annual installments, depending on the plan's rules. Taxes are deferred on contributions and earnings until the money is withdrawn at retirement. Many people receive their benefits as a lump sum and roll that over into an individual retirement account (IRA) in order to continue deferring taxes. Consult a tax advisor or accountant if you'd like more information on taxes and retirement income.

Probably the most popular example of defined-contribution plans is the 401(k). These plans had about 50 million participants in 2002, compared with 10 million in 1985.[2] Despite their growth, 401(k) plans have no guarantees that a specific amount will be paid out. Generally, employees are offered a choice of investment options—

including company stock—but it's up to them to decide where to invest their money. One feature of these accounts is that people can borrow money from them and later pay it back with interest to their own account. However, if a loan is taken and the borrower loses their job or quits, the money must be paid back immediately with interest, or else taxes and penalties must be paid.

Profit sharing is another type of defined-contribution plan in which employees get contributions based upon a percentage of a company's profits. However, if a company performs poorly there may be little profit to share. Employees may also have the option of adding money to these plans, which are paid out as a lump sum. Other defined-contribution plans are available for those who are self-employed or work for the government, schools, or nonprofits. Check with your employer for the specific details of any of these plans that may apply to your situation.

Saving for retirement isn't limited to employee-sponsored plans. IRAs can be opened by anyone who earns taxable income during the year (including salaries, tips, bonuses, and taxable alimony). Both spouses in a marriage can open an IRA even if one doesn't work and the working spouse funds both accounts. Money in IRAs can be put into a variety of investments. Two of the most popular are the traditional IRA and the Roth IRA.

Traditional IRA contributions and earnings aren't taxable until money is withdrawn at retirement. Early withdrawals are taxed and may require payment of a 10 percent penalty. The amount of a person's income and whether or not they participate in an employee-sponsored retirement plan determines if contributions are tax deductible. There is no minimum on how much can be put into an IRA, but as of 2003, an individual can contribute up to $3,000 annually with the potential to be eligible for a tax deduction. That amount will reach $5,000 by 2008. As of 2003 people fifty and over can make an additional catch-up contribution of $500 and that will rise to $1,000 in 2006.

Roth IRA contributions aren't deductible, but qualified distributions won't be taxed. Qualified distributions include those made after the account has been open for at least five years *and* the recipient is fifty-nine-and-a-half, disabled, or meets certain requirements as a first-time home buyer. Depending upon the circumstances, nonqualified distributions may be taxed as part of your gross income plus an additonal 10 percent penalty for early withdrawal. Check with your financial advisor to determine if you meet the income guidelines to open a Roth, or get a copy of the Internal Revenue Service publication *Individual Retirement Arrangements* (IRAs).

While it may be tempting to ignore retirement accounts once you've set up a schedule of regular contributions, it's important to monitor their progress regularly. Financial markets fluctuate constantly so money invested in securities is at the mercy of these changes. And if too much is invested in an employers' stock, there's a chance that retirement funds will be lost if the company has financial difficulties. Thousands of employees at Houston energy firm Enron discovered just how susceptible their retirement funds were to the company's financial instability in 2001 when they lost nearly $1 billion of their 401(k) savings, much of it invested in Enron shares. Having a diversified mix of cash, stocks, and bonds helps avoid being overinvested in any one sector.

Finally, be sure to read through any plan literature so that you truly understand the rules. Avoid just going along with recommendations from your financial advisor that you don't understand. It's your future and you want to be sure you're making informed, responsible decisions in planning for it.

Prayer Box

Dear Lord, thank you for allowing me to plan ahead for my future. I want to make informed choices when choosing how to handle my resources for retirement. I will work harder to be more disciplined with money in order to save. Please help me to have a vision for the future and believe that I will be blessed exceedingly and abundantly. Amen.

Tithing and Giving

Honor the LORD with your wealth, with the firstfruits of all your crops; then your barns will be filled to overflowing, and your vats will brim over with new wine.

Proverbs 3:9–10

Linda considers the act of giving to be one of her gifts. Although she says it's difficult for her to receive gifts, she enjoys blessing others with whatever she can share. "I'm very frugal for myself but am generous with other people . . . I like to bless people that way," she says. "God blesses us if we give our tithes and offerings with joy." She believes those blessings are evident in her life and are directly related to her giving. Not only does her job at a pharmaceutical company provide generous benefits such as profit sharing, but she has a low level of credit card debt and owns her town house.

In addition to tithes and offerings, Linda says her giving has involved charities such as United Way. When someone who does missions work asked her to support Campus

Crusade for Christ, she didn't hesitate. "I saw that this girl was sincere about what she wanted to do," says Linda. "Sometimes people will ask me [to give] and sometimes it depends on a need someone will have."

Linda is following the principle of giving outlined in Proverbs 3:27–28, "Do not withhold good from those who deserve it, when it is in your power to act. Do not say to your neighbor, 'Come back later; I'll give it tomorrow'—when you now have it with you." She has made giving as much a part of her life as writing a check to pay her bills. But many people find it difficult to incorporate giving into their financial picture.

> Look at the role of tithing and giving in your life. Address any misgivings about tithing and set up a plan to consistently make giving a part of your life.

"I'll tithe when I make more money," many people tell themselves. They have some vague idea of how much they need to earn before they can commit to tithing or giving money to charitable causes. Often that threshold continues to rise as they take on more debt and other financial obligations, and somehow they never get around to making room in their lives for giving. These people miss the point that tithing is the process of offering back to God a tenth of what he has given to us. It's giving the firstfruits of the resources he has blessed us with and is not the same as deciding to write a check for a new computer or television.

Being obedient to the Lord means giving tithes willingly and joyfully and trusting that he will bring blessings into your life because of your act. The poor widow who put two small copper coins that were worth less than a penny into the temple treasury was noticed by Jesus because of the sacrifice she made. Others who were wealthier put in much larger amounts, but the Lord knew the extent of the sacrifice she'd made with her small contribution. "Calling his disciples to him, Jesus said, 'I tell you the truth, this poor widow has put more into the treasury than all the others. They all gave out of their wealth; but she, out of her poverty, put in everything—all she had to live on'" (Mark 12:43–44). God knows what we are capable of giving, even if we deny him of it.

Paying What's Owed

Lengthy debates often occur about whether or not the tithe means 10 percent of your gross or net income. Some will argue that because the IRS takes taxes off the top of their income that it's an additional burden to have to tithe off the gross. But Scripture doesn't say that taxes take priority over tithing. It does instruct us to pay our taxes, as in Matthew 22:21 when Jesus was speaking to the Pharisees: "Then he said to them, 'Give to Caesar what is Caesar's, and to God what is God's.'" Just because many of us get taxes taken out of our pay before even receiving a check doesn't mean that we are to cheat God out of what he's owed.

Are you cheating God out of what he's due? Do you look for the smallest bill in your wallet to put into the offering plate? Maybe you feel justified in not tithing because you think that all of your hard-earned money will go nowhere but to pay for the pastor's new Lexus. Perhaps you do tithe regularly, but deep inside you resent having to give over that money. Maybe you don't go to church partly because of your reluctance to give.

If you have an attitude problem regarding tithing, ask God to open your heart and fill it with a generous spirit. Ask for forgiveness for being stingy with your money and for withholding what he gave you in the first place. After all, tithing is about your obedience to him, not what others may or may not be doing. If you've been overly judgmental about how the leadership in your church is spending money because it isn't what *you* would do with the funds, pray for more understanding and a willingness to obey God despite those differences.

If you genuinely believe that the leadership is irresponsible with the tithes and offerings, then you should pray about that, too. Perhaps you and other sisters in the church can spend some time praying together about the church's finances and leadership. Pastoral leaders can and do make mistakes, and they need as much prayer and support as they can get from members so they'll continue to make godly, wise decisions. Maybe you know someone in your congregation who is knowledgeable about financial planning and can volunteer to teach other members and help improve the situation.

Obviously you shouldn't look the other way if there are serious financial problems in your church or if the leadership truly is making ungodly decisions about the money. But while your first impulse may be to stop giving or to flee that church for another, be honest with yourself and ask if you've tried to help improve the situation or have just gossiped about it and watched judgmentally from afar. "A perverse man stirs up dissension, and a gossip separates close friends" (Prov. 16:28).

Why You Give

Think about your motives for giving. Does it make you feel special and important that you're able to give money at your church or to other charities? Do you look for praise and validation when giving money or get angry when others don't notice how much you've sacrificed?

One of the most amazing stories of selfless giving involves an elderly African-American woman named Oseola Mc-Carty who spent most of her life washing other people's laundry for low wages. McCarty, who lived very frugally in Hattiesburg, Mississippi, stunned the world in 1995 when at the age of 87 she donated her life savings of $150,000 to fund scholarships for black students at the University of Southern Mississippi—a school she'd never visited nor could have attended as a young woman. McCarty, who dropped out of the sixth grade to work and care for her sick grandmother, never married or had children but wanted to see other young people have the educational opportunities she never had.

"I wanted to share my wealth with the children," said Miss McCarty, whose only real regret is that she never went back to school. "I never minded work, but I was always so busy, busy. Maybe I can make it so the children don't have to work like I did."[1] McCarty's gift spurred local business leaders to match her donation and others to contribute to the fund. Despite all the media attention and other appearances that followed, McCarty never really seemed to understand what all the fuss was about. She died at age 91 and always remained humble about what simply became known as "The Gift."

People of all incomes are reaching into their pockets to help various causes despite ups and downs in the economy. People of all incomes are reaching into their pockets to help various causes despite ups and downs in the economy. In 2004, Americans gave $248.52 billion to philanthropy. The biggest portion, or $88.3 billion, went to religious organizations, while $33.84 billion went to education.[2]

Mission Statement

Decide how important tithing and giving is to you and draft a mission statement. How does it make you feel to know that you do or do not give to others? Do you have hidden agendas linked to your giving, such as becoming the head of a certain committee in your church? Maybe you've been the recipient of charity at some point in your life and that makes you more inclined to give. If you haven't looked at giving in the proper perspective, ask God to help you change your attitude and open your heart to helping others. "He who oppresses the poor shows contempt for their Maker, but whoever is kind to the needy honors God" (Prov. 14:31).

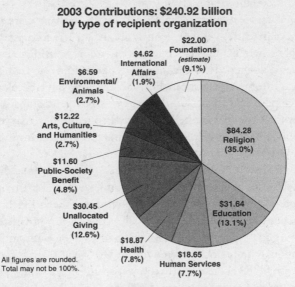

2003 Contributions: $240.92 billion by type of recipient organization

$22.00 Foundations *(estimate)* (9.1%)

$4.62 International Affairs (1.9%)

$6.59 Environmental/ Animals (2.7%)

$12.22 Arts, Culture, and Humanities (2.7%)

$11.60 Public-Society Benefit (4.8%)

$30.45 Unallocated Giving (12.6%)

$18.87 Health (7.8%)

$18.65 Human Services (7.7%)

$84.28 Religion (35.0%)

$31.64 Education (13.1%)

All figures are rounded. Total may not be 100%.

Source: AAFRC Trust for Philanthropy/*Giving USA 2003*

Figure 13.1

107

If you feel that you don't make enough money to tithe or give in other ways but truly feel this is important, then focus on getting to this point. Perhaps you need to adjust your routine when you get your paycheck. Consider your tithe to be as important as any other financial obligation you have instead of putting it at the bottom of the list. Try writing your tithe check first and living on whatever is left over, instead of the other way around. This may be difficult in the beginning, but if you make it a priority and really work at adjusting your spending, it will become easier. If you already tithe regularly and want to take your giving to the next level, then add an extra amount for an offering that is above and beyond your tithe.

Besides supporting your local church, perhaps there are certain causes you feel strongly about, such as feeding the poor, helping disaster victims, or providing housing to battered women. There are thousands of charities out there all eager for your donations, but before writing out a check to support them, make sure that the work they do is compatible with your values and beliefs. Is there an organization that you support because of its work in certain areas but that is involved in legislative activity that goes against your values?

Find organizations that have independent boards and that will be accountable for their operations, says Dan Busby, vice president for member and donor services at the Evangelical Council for Financial Accountability (ECFA) in Winchester, Virginia. "There should be a willingness to be transparent about their financial operations," he says. Charities affiliated with ECFA are required to conduct an independent audit by a certified public accountant each year, in addition to meeting state and federal guidelines. The Donor's Bill of Rights in figure 13.2 outlines other things to look for when giving to charities.

Donor's Bill of Rights

You have the right to:

- Know how the funds of an organization are being spent.
- Know what the programs you support are accomplishing.
- Know that the organization is in compliance with federal, state and municipal laws.
- Restrict or designate your gifts to a particular project.
- A response to your inquiries about finances and programs.
- Visit office and program sites of an organization to talk personally with the staff.
- Give without being high-pressured by the organization.
- Know that the organization is well managed.
- Know that there is a responsible governing board and know who those board members are.
- Know that all appeals for funds are truthful and accurate.

Evangelical Council for Financial Accountability

Figure 13.2

You also can request an annual report and financial statements from any organization to which you're considering giving money. If they are unwilling to comply with your request, move on to the next organization. The Better Business Bureau Wise Giving Alliance web site (www.give.org) will allow you to access reports on charities.

Once you've decided which groups you'd like to donate to, decide how much you can allocate toward your giving plan and write that figure in your mission statement. Even if you can only afford to give $25 a month to your favorite charity, that's a start. Over time, as you improve your financial situation, you'll be able to adjust the amount you put toward philanthropy. Many employers offer matching gifts programs for eligible charities, so check with your benefits office to see if this is an option. Never give cash, and make checks payable to the organization, not the individual soliciting donations. Keep receipts for contributions, which might be deductible on your tax return. If you have further questions about which donations qualify for deductions, visit www.irs.gov.

Prayer Box

Lord, help me to have a more generous spirit. I want to be faithful in my tithing and giving. Please clean my heart of any wrong attitudes or ideas I may have about giving. I understand that my tithes are a firstfruits offering to you. Help me to see this area as a positive way to impact others who may genuinely be in need. I want to be an obedient and faithful servant who gives humbly and joyfully. Amen.

How Do You Feel about Investing?

So if you have not been trustworthy in handling worldly wealth, who will trust you with true riches? And if you have not been trustworthy with someone else's property, who will give you property of your own?

Luke 16:11–12

When it comes to investing, 41-year-old Lala says she sticks with what she knows: real estate. She's confident that the six-unit apartment building that she purchased with her two siblings will be a good long-term investment with less risk than the stock market. Lala, who also bought a studio in a co-op, says she's watched her parents invest in rental properties since she was a child and has learned a lot over the years while helping them with maintenance and repairs. By splitting the duties associated with the apartment building, all three siblings are able to actively participate in managing their investment. "I feel confident about retirement

> **Evaluate your attitudes and beliefs about investing money. Determine what your goals and expectations are for investing. Seek godly counsel when making decisions.**

. . . Having rental property helps me always feel like I'll have a place to live," she says.

Lala considers herself a conservative investor who stays on familiar ground and generally avoids other types of investments. She has a retirement fund through her job but tends to rely on the financial advisor assigned to her account to make most of the decisions about it. She admits that she hasn't spent much time monitoring her investments since the initial meeting twenty years ago when she opened the account. Only as she began losing money when the soaring stock market of the '90s ran out of steam did she become concerned.

But even though there's a lot she could learn about stocks and mutual funds, Lala says she's never taken a class on investing (although she did take one on real estate) and isn't sure that she would. "I guess I've shied away from [investing in the markets] because I think it's too difficult. Maybe if someone I knew encouraged me I might."

Dealing with Risk

Knowing your tolerance for risk, or the safety of an investment, and understanding exactly what you're putting money into are crucial when setting up an investment plan. While Lala should take some time to become more familiar with how her retirement funds work and be more active in managing them, she's smart not to become overly invested in the stock market without understanding how it works.

Many investors who lost piles of money on Internet stocks paid little attention to those companies' bottom lines. Venture capitalists, bankers, and investors threw money at dot-coms without even knowing exactly what they did. Caught up in the euphoria that surrounded the markets during much of the '90s, many of these people ignored the fact that most of these companies had never turned a profit and were being highly valued largely because they had dot-com behind their names. The lesson here: Avoid investing in things you don't understand and do careful research before handing over your money.

If you'd like help with managing your money and making wise decisions, seek advice from people who are knowledgeable. "Plans fail for lack of counsel, but with many advisors they succeed" (Prov. 15:22). Talk with a financial advisor, pastoral counselor, family members, or friends who are trustworthy, informed, and display godly behavior when managing money. About 37 percent of female investors say financial advisors are their single most important source of advice about investing. The higher their net worth, the more likely they are to use advisors.[1]

Knowing what's happening to your money is your responsibility, so don't let the advice others give be a substitute for learning as much as possible from financial books, magazines, classes, or workshops at your church. Also, getting good counsel doesn't mean relying on the folks on your job who are always broke but somehow seem to dish out plenty of advice about how to handle money. "Stay away from a foolish man, for you will not find knowledge on his lips" (Prov. 14:7).

When shopping for a financial advisor, ask whether their services are fee based or whether they charge commissions on each sale. "The financial industry has a lot of salespeople trying to sell their one product, and that may keep people from using planners," says Christina V. Winch of Winch Advisory Services in Appleton, Wisconsin. When using a financial planner, it's important to regularly review the portfolio's strategy and discuss important life changes.

Write down how you feel about the concept of investing. Is this a topic you'd like to learn more about, or do you feel intimidated just thinking about it? Perhaps your eyes glaze over with boredom every time you see a financial report on TV. If you feel negatively about it, why do you suppose that is? Did your parents or some other family member tell you that investing should be avoided and you believed them? Do you feel that investing is only for rich people? Or maybe you're already comfortable investing money and want to make sure you're doing it according to God's principles.

Your Comfort Zone

Many women interviewed for this book had never taken a class about managing money but expressed an interest in learning more about investing and gaining more confidence to discuss financial topics with family and friends. Some even expressed discomfort with certain types of investing for reasons that included fear of losing hard-earned cash, not wanting to get caught up in a worldly focus on money or gambling mentality, and economic instability.

"A healthy approach is that we are in the world and not of it so why not use the world's system to our advantage and with wisdom," says counselor Trudy Colflesh. "There are conservative ways to invest. I don't think Christians should be naïve, but they should be wise. If we use the world's system we should realize the risk and not go overboard."

While there are many people who treat investing as just another get-rich-quick scheme and will do almost anything for their love of money, that's not the view the Creator intends for us to have. "The wages of the righteous bring them life, but the income of the wicked brings them punishment" (Prov. 10:16). Quitting a steady, well-paying job to day-trade or participate in some half-baked investment scheme with shady acquaintances is a recipe for disaster. Such a misplaced focus on amassing a large fortune puts money in the place of honor instead of God, creating a form of idolatry.

"You have to have a commitment to something in the community. Then you have a reason for all the money you're saving and have a legacy for your life," says Winch. "There are people with lots of money who are terribly unhappy. I don't know if they see a reason for what they're doing and how they're living."

There are numerous biblical references that give instruction on handling money and resources with traits such as honesty, humility, generosity, and faithfulness. King Solomon, blessed with incredible knowledge and staggering wealth, shared some of his wisdom about handling money in the books of Proverbs and Ecclesiastes. Make time to read through these books soon to study some of these nuggets of wisdom.

In Matthew 25, Jesus tells a parable about a master who entrusted three of his servants to watch over portions of his treasure until he returned from a trip. The first two servants put their money to work and doubled it. Pleased by their work, the master rewarded them for being faithful stewards over the money they were given by putting them in charge of even more resources. But the third, fearful of losing what he was given, hid it in the ground. Upon hearing this, the master was displeased and told him that he should have at least deposited it with the bankers to earn interest. "For everyone who has will be given more, and he will have an abundance. Whoever does not have, even what he has will be taken from him" (Matt. 25:29).

Each of us has been given a certain amount of resources that we are to be good and faithful stewards over. While not everyone has the same amount of money, we're all responsible for using and maintaining what we have in a mature way. So whether you have $100 or $100,000 in your bank account, the Lord wants you to manage that responsibly according to his principles.

Sticking with Principles

If you have concerns about investing in a socially responsible way and are working with an advisor, let them know this. "There are some socially responsible investing funds that are very good and some are not," says Winch, who during her years as a financial advisor has seen clients ask to avoid investments related to wars, smoking, abortion, and apartheid. "Each person has issues and you address them individually."

Write down a goal statement for what you would like to accomplish through an investing plan. This could be an extension of other financial goals you've already stated, or completely different. These goals might include taking an investing class, reading through Scripture passages about money, or subscribing to a personal finance magazine. Maybe you'd like to invest in mutual funds so that you can save enough to cover future college costs. Or perhaps you're more interested in buying rental properties and investing money in your cousin's new invention. Being an investor doesn't mean that you're limited to buying stocks. Think about honest, godly ways that you can manage your resources to get the best return on your money over the long term.

Regardless of whether you're looking to improve an existing investment strategy or hoping to begin one, have you paid off any credit card debt and set aside enough to cover your living expenses for several months in the event of an emergency? If not, you shouldn't be focused on investing at this time because you still have cleaning to do in your financial house. While you're taking care of these things, learn as much as possible about different types of investments in order to be prepared when the time is right.

If you've done those things and have disposable income to spare, decide how much risk you can tolerate. Are you willing to put money into investments and not get overly stressed-out if they fluctuate in value over time? Or are you the type who goes online several times a day to check your portfolio because you're afraid of losing even a few dollars? Do you have other financial obligations that would suffer if you lost the invested funds, such as putting more capital into a growing business? Do you have a past addiction to gambling that might cloud your judgment when making investment decisions?

Thinking through your motives and expectations for investing money will help establish clear goals. Avoid getting caught up in the hype of flavor-of-the-moment investments others might be involved with if they don't line up with God's Word. There are many investments out there that are simply get-rich-quick schemes targeting people's greed. We're blessed to enjoy the resources we've been given on this earth and should make good decisions about managing them, but in the end our real reward will be in heaven. "For the love of money is a root of all kinds of evil. Some people, eager for money, have wandered from the faith and pierced themselves with many griefs" (1 Tim. 6:10).

Prayer Box

Lord, help me to become better educated about ways to grow my money. I want to make godly investments that help me manage the resources I've been given. I don't want to get caught up in a get-rich-quick mentality or allow making money to consume me. I pray that my financial needs will be met, allowing me to follow the calling that I've been given. Amen.

Building a Portfolio

Give portions to seven, yes to eight, for you do not know
what disaster may come upon the land.

Ecclesiastes 11:2

Have you ever gotten excited about a promise someone
made to you? Imagine that a friend promised to give
you something or do a favor that would really help
you out of a difficult situation. Excited, you begin to dream
about all the blessings that will follow. Because you have
no reason to doubt that person will fulfill their promise,
you behave as if it's already a done deal and begin making
further plans. You even make a couple of commitments to
others because of your confidence in that pledge. Unable
to contain your enthusiasm, you share your situation with
family and friends.

Finally, when the big day arrives to receive what was promised, you can barely wait to see your friend and thank her for
such generosity. Only, when you go meet her, she sheepishly
informs you that she won't be able to follow through on

> **Diversify your investment mix. Evaluate your choices to decide if they're right for your situation. Understand how different investments work and choose wisely.**

her commitment. Disappointed and embarrassed, you realize you had put all your eggs in this one basket without making any backup plans. Even worse, now you'll have to break the promises *you* made to others because of counting on this one thing.

By not diversifying a portfolio, an investor is taking a huge gamble with their investment funds. They may count on earning money in one way, and if that fails they are left scrambling to pick up the pieces. Diversifying is simply putting money into different types of accounts or investments in order to cut down the amount of risk. A person who owns a mix of mutual funds, bonds, money market funds, and real estate has a better chance of weathering ups and downs in the economy than someone who only invests in the stock of one company.

It's important to choose investments you're comfortable with so that you aren't losing sleep every night thinking about them. If you currently have investments that constantly worry you or just don't feel right, then you should probably look at rebalancing your mix or even moving that money elsewhere. Pray before making big decisions about investing so that you are led to make good choices. "And my God will meet all your needs according to his glorious riches in Christ Jesus" (Phil. 4:19).

Investment Checklist

Look at your investing mission statement again. Think about existing and potential investments in relation to the following characteristics: risk, cost, return, and taxes. What is the risk of the investment, meaning how safe is it? Avoid putting money into something based only on a hot tip from your brother's friend's cousin without doing further research. Savings accounts and CDs are FDIC insured up to $100,000, but stocks aren't. Be aware of what could happen to the money you invest if there are problems later.

Although the two are related, risk differs from volatility, which is how much the cost of an investment varies over time. Stocks are very volatile and their prices can fluctuate dramatically during the course of just one day. The more volatile an investment the riskier it is. Be realistic about what you can tolerate and don't let others talk you into something that will make you uncomfortable. Good advisors will help you make decisions that don't compromise your beliefs or expose you to unnecessary risk.

How much will the investment cost, and can you really afford it? In addition to the initial purchase price, there may be fees or broker charges, and later, taxes. The minimum amount required to buy a savings bond isn't as much as it is to buy most mutual funds. To the beginning investor, the savings bond may seem like a better deal because the up-front costs are less, but looking at the long term, the mutual fund is likely to earn more money. Also, avoid taking cash advances on credit cards to pay for investments, no matter how much of a sure thing they seem to be. Not only will you build up more debt, but any interest earned on the investment is probably going to be less than the interest paid on the card.

Return is how much you can expect to earn on an investment. Often the more risky it is, the more potential there is to make larger amounts of money. Many people hope to earn regular income from their investments, particularly as they age and prepare to retire from the workplace. If generating income is important to you, it's important to choose long-term investments that have this potential. While most people would like to earn a decent return on their investments and not lose what they've put into them, it's important to avoid a mentality of instant gratification. Just because something may earn a lot of money quickly doesn't mean it's a good choice for you.

With many investments, past performance can be an indicator of how well they may perform in the future. For example, financial newspapers and magazines run tables showing how well mutual funds have performed over certain periods of time, and many investors rely on these track records when building a portfolio. Although this information can be very helpful, it shouldn't be the sole criteria for buying a mutual fund. The stock market is unpredictable and can change quickly based upon any number of unknown factors, including the latest economic news, corporate bankruptcies, or war.

The return on an investment also can be affected by taxes. The gains on the sale of any taxable investments will have to be reported to the IRS as part of your income. Gains on tax-exempt investments don't have to be reported. Often the higher a person's income and tax bracket, the more important it becomes to find investments that are tax exempt or deductible. Keep records of any investments you purchase or sell for a profit or loss so that you will be able to document deductions on your tax return. If you need more information about the tax consequences of your investments, consult an accountant or tax attorney.

Understanding Securities

When considering an investment strategy, consider your age and how soon you'll need access to the money. Generally, the closer to retirement you get, the less risk you'll want to assume. Savings accounts, CDs, and money market funds are low-risk investments because you'll get back the principal you put in even if interest rates are low. Cash that needs to remain liquid can be kept in money market funds, which aren't 100 percent risk-free but usually have better interest rates than basic savings accounts.

Bonds are fixed income investments that are more risky than money market funds but less so than stocks. Bonds are debt securities where the money invested is being lent to a government entity or company in exchange for a fixed interest rate. That interest is either paid at specific times over the life of the bond or when it matures. The principal is repaid when the bond matures.

Treasury securities are issued by the federal government and their earnings are exempt from state and local income taxes. Federal taxes can be deferred until bonds reach final maturity or until they're redeemed. Treasury bills mature in terms ranging from a few days to twenty-six weeks, notes mature in two to ten years, and bonds mature in more than ten years. Each requires a minimum investment of $1,000. Savings bonds can be bought for as little as $25. The money can't be redeemed until six months after the bond is issued, and early redemption penalties will be imposed if it's held less than five years. For information on Treasuries, go to the U.S. Department of Treasury web site at www.treasury direct.gov.

Municipal bonds are issued by local and state governments to pay for public projects, and the income produced is usually exempt from federal taxes. Corporate bonds are issued by companies looking to raise money and have high risk because they're backed only by that entity. Interest from these investments is taxable. To cut down on the amount of risk from these types of investments, many investors purchase shares of bond mutual funds that invest in a variety of securities.

Mutual funds are attractive to people who don't want to spend a lot of time monitoring individual investments. They invest in a variety of stocks or bonds, reducing the likelihood of losing all of an investment if a company goes under, and a manager oversees the fund. The load is the percentage of the investment that is charged for buying shares of a fund and other fees for maintaining it. No-load funds don't require a fee for purchasing shares but may have redemption fees, which are charged when shares are sold. Some funds also charge 12b-1 fees, which help pay for advertising and marketing costs. Before buying a mutual fund ask for a copy of the prospectus, which will answer many questions about the fund's strategy, companies invested in, and other financial information (see figure 15.1).

Potential Risk of Mutual Fund Types

High Risk
International Stock
Industry Specific Stock
More Aggressive Stock
General Stock
Balanced
Long-Term Bond
Intermediate-Term Bond
Short-Term Bond
Money Market
Low Risk

Portions excerpted from Vanguard.com with permission of The Vanguard Group, Inc.

Figure 15.1

Companies that issue stocks also issue prospectuses and annual reports that give details about their businesses, leadership, and earnings. All of these reports should be examined when deciding whether to buy stocks, which are shares in a company. By purchasing shares of common stock in a publicly held company, you're eligible to vote as a shareholder. Some stocks pay dividends, which are a percentage of the company's profits that are mailed out in a check to the shareholder or can be reinvested to buy additional shares. Stocks can be risky but have the potential to appreciate quickly. Whether you choose to buy individual stocks or mutual funds, getting a mix of blue-chips (the shares of larger, more established companies), medium, and small stocks can help spread some of the risk.

With any investments it's best to buy for the long term. Don't worry so much about trying to time your decisions to movements in the stock market or to political instability. By making regular contributions to accounts, you can take advantage of dollar cost averaging. For example, if you put $100 into a mutual fund every month, you'll buy shares at whatever the market price is at the time. Because the market fluctuates, your $100 will buy more shares when the price is lower and fewer shares when the price is higher.

Decide which types of investments are right for you. Consult the financial pages of your local newspaper and look at a couple of personal finance magazines to get more information on specific investments. Look at some of the personal finance web sites listed in appendix A to learn more about managing a portfolio.

Request information from several financial firms that allow you to open investment accounts or purchase securities. If you have a financial planner, they can help narrow down your choices and set up an investing account. Be sure to understand the types of service you'll get and any fees involved. Expect to pay higher fees with a full-service firm that takes a more active role in managing your portfolio, as opposed to a discount broker that expects you to do more of the decision making. Appendix C has a listing of some financial firms.

Prayer Box

Dear Lord, thank you for giving me access to so many resources that can help me manage my finances better and have the means to advance the work of your kingdom. Let your wisdom guide the choices I make about how to invest money. I don't want to take unnecessary risk but want to choose wise investments that will make my money grow. Allow me to have patience and discipline in this area. Amen.

Technology and Money

For wisdom will enter your heart, and knowledge will be pleasant to your soul. Discretion will protect you, and understanding will guard you. Wisdom will save you from the ways of wicked men, from men whose words are perverse.

Proverbs 2:10–12

Technology has changed the way we make, spend, and manage money. Long gone are the days when people had to make weekly trips to a bank and stand in long lines, waiting to deposit paychecks or withdraw money. Not only is it now common for many customers to exclusively use ATMs, but many banks are also charging for the privilege of getting service from a live teller. Amazon, eBay, and other web sites are a regular stop for many shoppers looking for a bargain from the comfort of their own home.

And remember the infamous day traders during the stock market boom of the '90s? Many of these people quit paying

> **Examine the influence of technology on financial transactions in society. Become more knowledgeable about using computers and the Internet. Guard against potential fraud.**

jobs to spend their days at home buying and selling stocks online. Unfortunately, the lure of making millions caught up with many of these folks who had relied on Internet companies to sustain them, and they ended up losing much of the wealth they had amassed on paper —as well as being hit with big tax bills—when the stock market headed south.

Even with the demise of many Internet companies, new ones are taking their place, and electronic and online financial transactions continue to gain in popularity. An estimated 21 million households in the U.S. used the Internet for banking in 2002, and that figure is expected to climb to 43 million by 2006.[1] Getting a boost from the online auction business, more than 100 million electronic payments exchanged hands in 2002, with a large portion of them handled by PayPal, a company that allows people to e-mail money to bank accounts and other individuals. These transactions, known as p-to-p payments, are expected to grow to 4 billion by 2005, and many financial companies are looking for ways to get in on the action.[2] Eventually, many finance experts continue to speculate, our society will operate completely on a paperless monetary system.

24-Hour Access

In many ways changes in technology have made it simpler to manage money. Web sites provide a host of information on various topics related to money. Many financial transactions occur twenty-four hours a day online and at ATMs, making it more convenient and sometimes cheaper for people who have little time to spare on errands such as going to their brokerage. Money can even be quickly moved around the world with a phone call or the press of a computer button.

All this convenience comes at a price, however. With increased use of the Internet and electronic networks for handling financial transactions has come an increase in theft and fraud via these channels. Reaching live customer service representatives sometimes seems all but impossible. And the ease with which personal information is collected and sold has alarmed individuals concerned about privacy. Many folks are left wondering whether these technological advances are positive changes to be embraced or trouble to be avoided. Others allow fear to keep them from gaining any knowledge about what's available to them in this area or what should be monitored for safety purposes.

How knowledgeable are you about how the Internet and other electronic networks are involved in the financial system? Do you fear these changes and avoid having anything to do with them? Are you comfortable using computer software programs to keep track of your finances? Have you ever surfed the Web to research information on investing or biblical topics related to finance?

Write down your impressions about where technology fits into your financial goals. Would you like to become more comfortable researching information online, such as finding the best mortgage rates or auto deals in your area? Do you embrace change and enjoy learning new things? Or are you often intimidated by new technologies and as a result usually steer clear of them?

Don't let fear keep you from equipping yourself with useful tools and information that will help on your walk to better stewardship. Don't let what you've heard about the Internet keep you from accessing some of the positive resources that may help you. "I sought the LORD and he answered me; he delivered me from all my fears" (Ps. 34:4).

While you want to steer clear of any questionable financial schemes or information that contradicts Scripture, there is a host of resources that can be valuable in organizing your finances. Of course there are a variety of magazines and books on the market, but most of the resources discussed in this section involve using a computer. If you don't own a computer, you can probably gain access to one at your local public library, which may also have free Internet service.

Tap into the Web

First things first: computers are here to stay. If you've never used one, I highly suggest that you sign up for a free or low-cost computer class at your local community college or through an adult continuing education program. Some communities even offer special classes for senior citizens, students, and those with low incomes. If you can't find such a class, ask a computer-savvy relative or friend to give you a crash course. Don't use the excuse that you can't afford to learn computer skills and don't have the time or you'll continue to miss out on all kinds of great resources. Once you have Internet access, spend some time looking at some of the personal finance and other web sites listed in appendix A.

If you use financial calculators on web sites, you shouldn't be asked for personal information such as social security numbers or financial account numbers. Also, most companies don't send unsolicited e-mails asking you for personal information or credit card numbers. If you receive this kind of e-mail and it appears to be from a company you do business with, call the number you already have for customer service (not the one in the e-mail) and report it.

If you choose to open an account online or sign up for a service that requires using a credit card to make payments, then you may be asked for more specific information such as a billing address. However, if you're not comfortable giving personal information over the Internet, call the company to complete the transaction or request an application for opening an account or receiving service through good old-fashioned snail mail. If a web site offering financial services doesn't provide an address or phone number, then you may want to rethink signing up with them. Use common sense when doing any kind of business online and make sure you're comfortable that you know who you're dealing with.

If you're interested in banking online, ask if your bank offers this service and whether or not there's a charge. Many banks offer account access and basic transactions at no charge, but if you request bill payment services you may pay a monthly fee. Many credit card companies also have online payments, balance transfers, and monthly statements. Access to most online financial services usually requires setting up a password and PIN for security purposes.

Financial software programs such as Quicken and Microsoft Money are wonderful for managing home and small business finances. These programs must be installed on a computer and allow the user to keep track of bank accounts, investments, and credit cards, do estate planning, and set up a budget. If you find managing your finances a chore, these programs can really help simplify that task. While they don't require Internet access to use, these programs can link to Quicken and Microsoft web sites that offer additional planning tools, research, calculators, and portfolio trackers. They can also link to your financial accounts to import data into your computer.

Be Safe, Not Sorry

Because fraud and theft (Internet and non-Internet related) are on the rise, take precautions to avoid problems. While many web sites have extra security measures encrypted into them, hackers can and do occasionally find ways to get past them, so use prudence when purchasing items online with a credit card. Avoid using debit cards for online purchases since they link directly to your bank account. Also, only use ATMs for financial institutions that you're familiar with to avoid the possibility of phony machines set up to steal card numbers. If you see charges you didn't make on your bank or credit card statement, report it to the card issuer immediately and have it cancelled.

Identity theft is one of the fastest growing crimes in the U.S., and cost consumers about $5 billion and businesses nearly $48 billion in 2002, according to the Federal Trade Commission. Identity theft often involves stolen credit card and social security card numbers. Once a thief has access to this information, they may be able to obtain new cards, empty checking accounts, or even take out loans using the victim's name.

In late 2002, a large identity theft case was uncovered by authorities, who arrested a group of thieves for stealing at least $2.7 million from thirty thousand Americans using fraudulently obtained credit reports and laptop computers. And in May 2006, about 26.5 million veterans were placed at risk of identity theft when an electronic data file containing their names, birth dates, and social security numbers were stolen from the home of a Department of Veterans Affairs employee.

Online fraud can also involve unsolicited e-mails that prey upon people's emotions, lack of knowledge about a situation, or even greed. E-mail inboxes are flooded with charity solicitations accompanied by sad stories about sick children, appeals for prayer, and chain letters threatening bad luck if money isn't paid. If I had a dollar for every spam I get offering get-rich-quick business opportunities, asking me to help smuggle money out of politically unstable countries, and telling me I've won some sweepstakes I've never even heard of, I'd have a nice chunk of money to supplement my income!

Not only do such offers generally sound too good to be true, but trying to take advantage of them to make a quick buck isn't grounded in biblical wisdom. God wants us to be prosperous people, but not dishonestly. For many folks it's tempting to take advantage of questionable business or investment schemes because they're desperate for money. Christians who get involved in such schemes may even tithe off what they earn to try to make up for any wrongdoing. But yielding to such temptation opens the door to lying and subterfuge and will only lead to other problems later. "Woe to him who piles up stolen goods and makes himself wealthy by extortion! How long must this go on?" (Hab. 2:6).

Another fast-growing form of credit card fraud involves what's known as "skimming." That happens when a person who works as a store clerk, waiter, or bartender quickly swipes an unsuspecting customer's card through a hand-held scanner, allowing information on the card's magnetic strip to be recorded and later used by them or sold to a network of credit card forgers. Skimming is probably easiest to do at restaurants because the customer's card is often taken away from the table to be swiped. Watching the card as your order is processed is the best way to avoid this happening to you.

In the end, use common sense when dealing with your money. If something deep down inside doesn't feel right about a financial transaction, then it's probably best to avoid it. The Holy Spirit speaks to us in many ways about various situations in our lives and we need to be open to that. Since God wants to enlarge our territory, then surely the Holy Spirit intercedes at times to try to keep us from making bad financial decisions. "Do not set foot on the path of the wicked or walk in the way of evil men. Avoid it, do not travel on it; turn from it and go on your way. For they cannot sleep till they do evil; they are robbed of slumber till they make someone fall" (Prov. 4:14–16).

Prayer Box

Lord, thank you for giving me the resources to assist me on my financial makeover. I pray for wisdom and clarity when choosing to use the Internet and other information sources. Please guide me to information that lines up with your Word. I also ask that you would shield me from fraud and dishonest people. Amen.

Net Worth

You may say to yourself, "My power and the strength of my hands have produced this wealth for me." But remember the LORD your God, for it is he who gives you the ability to produce wealth, and so confirms his covenant, which he swore to your forefathers, as it is today.

Deuteronomy 8:17–18

How much money is enough? Talk show host Oprah Winfrey, whose entertainment empire is estimated to be worth nearly $1 billion, admitted that she once hoarded $50 million in cash, which she called her personal "bag-lady fund," because she's so uncomfortable investing her money in the stock market.[1] While that may seem incredible to many of us who will never see anywhere near that amount of money in our lifetimes, it underscores the fact that one person's sense of security may differ greatly from the next person's and has little to do with actual dollar amounts.

"Money unfortunately rules much of our lives," says Felicia Hairr, a former CPA who helped start the Women's

> Evaluate how money relates to feelings of security. Calculate your total net worth. View building net worth as a means to have more freedom to focus on your life's mission.

Financial Ministry at Perimeter Church in Atlanta. "But there's a difference between hoarding and saving. We have women who've accumulated more than they need but haven't come to a point where they trusted God and put the brakes on their lifestyle." Deciding not to upgrade to a bigger home you don't really need and cutting back on accumulating more things may be part of putting on the brakes. "A person should pray and look at their situation and see . . . what do I really need to live on?"

How much money do you think *you* need to live comfortably? Are you confident that the Lord will provide for your needs, or do you hoard what you get because deep down inside you really aren't sure about that? "People curse the man who hoards grain, but blessing crowns him who is willing to sell" (Prov. 11:26). If you're a hoarder, what is causing that type of bondage? Were you poor as a child, or are you still bailing out after declaring bankruptcy? Do you buy as much as you can—including things you really don't need—because you're fearful that at any time you may be unable to afford even the basics and you need to stock up?

Perception vs. Reality

Perhaps you believe in always buying the best and most expensive items in order to appear successful and prosperous. Many people believe that the wealthiest individuals in our society are the ones who wear the most expensive clothes, drive the flashiest cars, live in the most expensive homes, and party with the jet set. But the average American millionaire lives in a home valued at an average of $320,000, drives older model American cars, and wears inexpensive suits.[2] This flies in the face of the widespread belief that those with the most conspicuous consumption habits have the highest net worth. In fact, many high income individuals are living paycheck to paycheck, barely keeping their heads above water, and have little net worth.

Do you know what your net worth is? That's the amount you'd have if you sold all your assets and paid off all your debts. If you don't know your net worth and can't figure out why you're unable to stretch your paycheck and save money, then you may be living way beyond your means.

More than a quarter of American households surveyed had net assets of less than $10,000. In general these people were under 35, had low or moderate incomes, and rented their homes. Not only weren't they able to cover major emergencies without borrowing, but they probably couldn't afford to buy a home, pay for an education, or start a business. These people also tended to spend more than their incomes and didn't plan for the long term.[3]

Crunch the Numbers

Use the worksheet in figure 17.1 to calculate your net worth. (If you're married, calculate this amount for you and your spouse together.) To have an effective financial makeover you need to know this important piece of information, so don't skip this exercise. In order to know where you're going it's important to know where you are.

Net Worth

Assets	Value
Cash	
Checking accounts	
Savings accounts	
Money market accounts	
CDs	
Stocks	
Bonds	
Mutual funds	
Other investments	
Home	
Other homes	
Rental property	
Other real estate	
IRAs	
Retirement plan	
Other retirement plan	
Life insurance	
Personal property (furniture, clothing, auto, etc.)	
Antiques and collectibles	
Other	
Other	
Total Assets	

Liabilities	Amount Owed
Mortgage	
Other mortgages	
Auto loan	
Student loans	

Liabilities	Amount Owed
Other loans	
Credit cards	
Lines of credit	
Child support	
Alimony	
Other	
Other	
Total Liabilities	
Net Worth (Total Assets – Total Liabilities)	

Figure 17.1

Write down the amount of all your assets such as equity in your home, autos that have been completely paid for, expensive jewelry, or investments. Then write down the amount of all your liabilities, or what you owe to people. That may include credit cards, home equity loans, or child support payments. If the assets total more than liabilities, the difference is your net worth. If the amount of your liabilities is higher than your assets, then you have a negative net worth and have a lot of work to do to cut down that debt.

Calculate your net worth at least once a year so you'll have an accurate snapshot of your financial health. Having this information will help identify areas where you need to focus more of your attention, such as paying off a car loan.

Don't become so preoccupied with increasing net worth that you spend all your time working at the expense of your personal health and family time, or become greedy and miserly in your reluctance to give or spend on necessities.

Is it really necessary to work two jobs to provide for your family, or are you simply looking for a way to fund an overly lavish lifestyle? "Be shepherds of God's flock that is under your care, serving as overseers—not because you must, but because you are willing, as God wants you to be; not greedy for money, but eager to serve" (1 Peter 5:2).

The idea is not to spend large amounts of time and energy increasing your net worth just so you can be wealthy according to the world's standards, but is to have the financial means to pursue your mission in life. Think about all those volunteer projects in your church or community that you've always wanted to get involved with but have no time for because you work long hours to pay bills. Or maybe you've always wanted to start your own business but just can't seem to put enough money aside to have a financial cushion to leave your current job. Increasing net worth reflects a disciplined approach to managing money and can provide more freedom to contribute to God's kingdom. "'Come, follow me,' Jesus said, 'and I will make you fishers of men'" (Matt. 4:19).

Focusing more on serving others and fulfilling your purpose will ultimately be more satisfying than concentrating on the dollars in your bank account. The more time you spend worrying about how and when you'll become rich, the less time you'll have to devote to the things that really matter in life. And the overemphasis on getting big money can open you up to the temptations of making fast and easy money through questionable business schemes or gambling. As you take authority over your time and talents and begin to see them in the proper perspective, you'll be surprised at how your resources begin to multiply, increasing your net worth.

Despite what has occurred with your finances in the past, believe that you have the power to change and improve your situation. Don't let the baggage you may be carrying around keep you from enjoying all that God has in store for you. Reject the harmful words and actions of those who would try to encourage a spirit of poverty or victimization in you. If you have a lot of naysayers around you, pray for positive people to enter your life who will affirm and uplift you. In turn, encourage them as they, too, seek success and prosperity.

Prayer Box

Dear Lord, thank you for the time and talents that you have given me. I want to use them to glorify you, Father, and fulfill my purpose in life. By obeying your Word and being faithful in taking care of my finances, I believe that my net worth will be adequate to help with the needs of my household. I won't focus on getting rich, but will instead look to serve others. I will aim to be rich in the fruit of your Spirit. Amen.

Tax Savvy

But so that we may not offend them, go to the lake and throw out your line. Take the first fish you catch; open its mouth and you will find a four-drachma coin. Take it and give it to them for my tax and yours.

Matthew 17:27

Some people will do anything to get out of paying taxes. Claiming phony deductions, opening offshore bank accounts, and ignoring filing deadlines are just some of the ways people try to evade the IRS. Others don't engage in illegal behavior but procrastinate over filing returns because they resent owing tax to Uncle Sam or avoid this task as they do many other things in life. Go to any post office on April 15 and you'll see droves of these people lined up waiting to mail their tax returns.

The idea of paying taxes stirs up many feelings in people, including annoyance, dread, panic, and boredom. But whatever you think about this topic, the fact is that we're legally obligated to pay tax on earned income at federal, state, and sometimes local levels. And if we own property or buy goods and services, we're usually taxed on that, too. Not paying these taxes can result in fines or even jail time.

All those taxes can really add up. The higher your income, the higher your tax bracket, or the percentage of your income that goes to taxes. But paying taxes doesn't have to be a big headache. With careful planning and organization you may be able to cut your tax bill and keep more of your income for other purposes. An approaching April 15 deadline shouldn't be the only thing that gets you thinking about your taxes. Incorporating legal tax reduction strategies into all areas of your financial planning will not only make things easier when you file a return, but also help you better manage your money overall.

> Plan tax strategies to make the most of your hard-earned pay. Organize and prepare paperwork for filing your annual return. Avoid trouble with the IRS.

Adjust Tax Withholding

If you feel you're paying too little or too much in taxes, then you may need to adjust your withholding using IRS Form W-4. Many people like the idea of getting a tax refund each year, but by adjusting the amount of tax withheld from their paychecks, they would end up with more take-home pay. Doing this would decrease the amount of any refunds, which are essentially no-interest loans to the government of taxpayer funds. However, be careful when adjusting withholding so that you don't underpay your taxes. If you do get a refund, use it to pay down debt or build up savings.

Adjust the number of personal allowances you're claiming on the W-4 if your family situation has changed. You're allowed to claim yourself and any dependents you support financially. The more dependents you claim, the less tax that's withheld. If you're a divorced or separated parent and share custody of children, make sure you discuss this with your former spouse since only one of you can claim the same dependent.

If you're self-employed, you'll want to make estimated tax payments on a quarterly basis so that you aren't hit with a huge bill at the end of the year. Since you're responsible for paying your own taxes to the government, you'll have to be especially diligent about organizing paperwork to document your situation. Self-employed individuals can claim many deductions for work-related expenses, so be sure to get the appropriate IRS publications about self-employment and take advantage of these items.

Deductions you may be able to claim if you're self-employed include business-related travel expenses, legal services, utility bills, and supplies. If you don't have evidence such as receipts or cancelled checks to back up these claims, leave them off your tax return because they will be challenged if you're audited by the IRS. Audits are simply detailed examinations of tax returns to make sure that enough tax was paid and that there's enough evidence to support any deductions. Returns claiming self-employment expenses are often red flags to the IRS when deciding who will be audited.

If you're planning to itemize deductions on a personal return, it's important to plan for them throughout the year by organizing appropriate paperwork. If deductions aren't itemized, you'll have to take the standard deduction, which may not be the best move for your situation. Deductions cannot be itemized on the Form 1040 EZ, so use Form 1040.

Among the items that can be deducted are certain work-related expenses that aren't reimbursed by your employer such as those for a home office, uniforms, union dues, and subscriptions to trade journals. Travel, meals, and vehicle-related costs are also eligible for deductions.

Also itemize non-job-related expenses such as charitable giving, IRA contributions, interest paid on home mortgage loans, and property taxes. Many people are surprised at how purchasing a home can make a big difference on their tax bill because of these deductions. Large medical expenses, tuition, and student loan interest may also be deductible. You can get forms and publications at www.irs.gov or call 1-800-TAX-FORM (1-800-829-3676). Also, if you are unsure about your options, consult an accountant or tax attorney.

Investment losses and gains also need to be reported to the government. Gains on the sale of investments have to be included as income, while losses can be deducted in the year they occur. If you're holding on to a stock that has steadily lost money, you may want to consider selling it and deducting the amount of your loss. While gains on certain investments such as savings bonds are exempt from state and local income taxes, gains on stock sales aren't. Your brokerage will report gains and losses to the IRS and send you a statement summarizing them at the end of the year.

To Tell the Truth

Be honest when itemizing deductions on your return. While it may be tempting to inflate the amount of deductions or not report income from certain sources such as tips or royalties, you're only going to harm yourself in the long run. Just one exaggeration or outright lie opens the door to more subterfuge, and before you know it you're scheming in all kinds of ways just to keep up with your stories. And if you do get audited, you'll have a tough time explaining the whole thing to the government.

Being in bondage to a lying spirit isn't fun and takes a lot of work. If you've been dishonest about your taxes (and other areas) in the past, pray for forgiveness and ask the Lord to help change this behavior. Write down how it makes you feel to be untruthful and why you do it. If you've been dishonest on your tax returns or have failed to file some of them, you need to correct this. You're better off owning up to your mistakes and setting up some sort of payment plan with the IRS than living in fear that you'll be caught at any time.

Also avoid any tax schemes that seem too good to be true such as methods to pay zero taxes on income, paying taxes to receive prizes, and special credits for African-Americans related to slavery. The IRS paid out more than $30 million in erroneous refunds in 2000 and 2001 to people seeking nonexistent reparation credits.[1] The government also identified 3,100 people who tried to evade $56 million of taxes from 1999 to 2001 by filing returns showing zero income and seeking the return of taxes their employers withheld.[2]

Unscrupulous tax preparers can also defraud you by diverting a portion of your refund to them or charging inflated fees for tax preparation services. Be careful who you choose to do business with. Just because someone sets up shop and says they prepare returns doesn't mean they're trustworthy. Ask them about their qualifications and whether or not you'll be able to go back to them in the event the return is audited. Also, never sign a return prepared by another individual without reviewing it carefully.

Don't wait until a week before your tax return is due to try to find help. If you have a complicated financial situation and need help from an accountant or tax preparer, ask for recommendations from family and friends. Check the person out and make sure you're comfortable with them having access to your personal information. If you feel confident about preparing your own tax return, invest in some tax-planning software for your computer. Don't forget to deduct the cost of software or other professional advice related to preparing returns.

If April 15 is a long way off, don't think that means you should neglect tax planning. Read through the tax publications you requested to better understand what applies to your situation. Set up folders to organize relevant paperwork such as receipts, cancelled checks, or acknowledgment letters from charities you support. Also keep tax returns and all supporting paperwork from the previous seven years in separate folders labeled by year. File your return and make any payments on time. If you can't meet that deadline, file an extension form, which will give you more time. Avoiding the situation will only delay your obligations and raise your stress level. Efficient preparation will help make tax time go more smoothly.

Prayer Box

Lord, thank you for your love and forgiveness in my life. Help me to be better organized about handling my taxes. I know that legally I am obligated to pay taxes and file a return, and I don't want to shirk this responsibility. I know that as I trim my tax bill, I will have more income to use for other purposes and will be responsible with that overflow. If I receive a tax refund, I will use it to pay debt or save as much of it as I can and not spend it frivolously. Amen.

All about Insurance

If anyone does not provide for his relatives, and especially for his immediate family, he has denied the faith and is worse than an unbeliever.

1 Timothy 5:8

Webster's dictionary defines the noun *insurance* as "coverage by contract whereby one party undertakes to indemnify or guarantee another against loss by a specified contingency or peril." The verb *insure* is defined as "to make certain especially by taking necessary measures and precautions." When Jesus Christ died on the cross for us over two thousand years ago, he paid the premium on the greatest insurance policy the world has ever known. Without that payment, we wouldn't have the promise of salvation. We've been given the precious gift of a binding contract that has been paid in full and entitles us to eternal life in God's kingdom. All we have to do is accept Jesus into our hearts as Lord and Savior.

Can you imagine what life would be like if Jesus hadn't died for our sins and entered such an awesome contract? It's hard to imagine, but one thing is for sure: No matter how difficult things may get, we'll always have this "life insurance" because of his sacrifice. "Now if we are children, then we are heirs—heirs of God and co-heirs with Christ, if indeed we share in his sufferings in order that we may also share in his glory" (Rom. 8:17).

> **Evaluate your insurance needs based upon your family situation and lifestyle. Make a list of current insurance policies you own.**

When you purchase insurance for you and your family—whether it's life, health, or auto—you're guaranteeing a form of protection in case of some unexpected event. Don't go without needed coverage because you want to avoid any talk about death and accidents or you just don't want to be bothered. Avoiding the issue isn't a responsible move and is a disservice to any dependents you may have. But with all of the different types of insurance policies out there it can be a little confusing to sort out what you do and don't need.

Fear Factor

One mistake many people make is purchasing insurance based on fear. They buy multiple insurance policies that they really don't need because they're so afraid of what may happen from day to day. Have you ever bought a new appliance and had the salesperson try to scare you into buying an extended warranty? You may even have declined the warranty at the store but a few weeks after making your purchase received another offer in the mail for the same coverage.

In the aftermath of 9-11 there has been an increased threat of more terrorist attacks and war, and it can be difficult to deal with the anxiety, stress, and confusion you may feel. But while these events may motivate you to get your financial affairs in order, don't allow fear or scare tactics to rule your decisions when choosing insurance or making other important life decisions. If you find that fear is clouding your judgment, pray for courage to confront this issue and correct it. Know that God is and will always be in control. "You will not fear the terror of night, nor the arrow that flies by day" (Ps. 91:5).

Another mistake people make with insurance is choosing policies based on what others around them need instead of on their own situation. Not everyone requires the same type or amount of coverage. Just because your coworker, who has three children, a mortgage, and a dog, has a $500,000 life insurance policy, doesn't mean you need one if you don't have any children, rent an apartment, and have no debt. But you will want to make sure you have adequate health and renter's insurance.

Have you obtained policies that accurately reflect your stage of life? Is it important to you to be adequately insured, or do you feel this is a waste of money? If you do have insurance, have you read through the policies so that you fully understand what kind of coverage you have? Do you know how long it would take for you or your family to actually collect on an insurance policy if necessary? Do you even know where the paperwork is for your policies?

Gather together any insurance policies you already own. Make a list of what kind of insurance it is and the amount of the premium that you pay for it. If you have more than one copy of a single policy, refer to the most recent one. Label file folders with each type of policy you have so that you can access them quickly (i.e., auto, disability, homeowner's). If you find that you have the same type of policy with two or more companies, then you might be overpaying for that area of coverage. Read through the policies carefully so that you will be able to decide whether it's more cost efficient for you to cancel any duplicate coverage.

Make sure you really understand what it means if you do cancel a policy. If you intend to buy another to replace it, wait until the new policy is in place so that you aren't left without coverage. Once you've thought this over carefully and have decided you really don't need a specific policy, write a letter to the insurer asking that it be cancelled and for a refund of any prepaid premiums.

Avoid Unnecessary Policies

There are some types of insurance you really don't need, such as those that cover accidents and specific diseases like cancer, because health insurance already covers those areas. Also, mortgage insurance, which pays off a mortgage if you die, and credit life insurance, which pays off credit cards and loans after your death, aren't necessary. If paying off these types of debt after your death is of concern to you, then make sure you have enough life insurance to cover them.

Watch out for all the offers from your credit card company for insurance policies in case you're unemployed or injured and can't pay your monthly bill. If you carry a balance, these policies often sound like a good deal because they may offer two or three months of free coverage before you have to pay a monthly fee. Once the trial period ends, however, the fee automatically gets charged to your card each month unless you notify the company to cancel it. In this case, skipping the credit card insurance, focusing on paying off any debts you owe, and building a savings is the best plan of action. Then, if you do suddenly lose your job or become injured, you won't have to worry about a lot of debt on top of other issues.

The Old Testament has numerous references to covenants being made between God and his people that promise future generations prosperity and favor. When God's children were obedient and honored these covenants, they were rewarded with their inheritance. But when they disobeyed and turned away from the Lord, they and/or their children suffered the consequences and often lost out on many of the blessings that would otherwise have been theirs. By getting your insurance needs in order, you are setting up the framework for you and your family to have the blessings that might be needed during an unexpected or difficult event.

Prayer Box

Lord, thank you for the awesome price you paid to save me. Because of you I have a life insurance policy that's paid in full and can never be cancelled. Help me to plan accurately for my insurance needs here on earth. I don't want to avoid this task and will take the necessary steps to be mature and responsible in this area. I know that by taking a little time now to do this, I will save myself some potential problems in the future. I give you my fears regarding insurance and pray that you guide me to get the adequate coverage that I need. Amen.

Getting Insurance

A good man leaves an inheritance for his children's children,
but a sinner's wealth is stored up for the righteous.

Proverbs 13:22

If you have health insurance through your employer or some
other group, then consider yourself blessed, even if getting
through to customer service is no picnic. About 45.8 million Americans don't have any health insurance, and many
of them are families headed by a working adult, according to
the U.S. Census Bureau. Being uninsured isn't just a problem
for the poor. In 2001, about 800,000 people with incomes
over $75,000 didn't have health insurance because they ei-
ther lost their jobs or were unable to afford high premiums.[1]
Many of these uninsured folks could probably tell stories
about the frustration and even embarrassment they suffer
at times when trying to obtain health care.

While purchasing an individual health insurance policy
is usually cost prohibitive for most people, there are some
options out there. If you're a member of a certain profession

153

> **Review various types of insurance available. Decide how much insurance you and/or your family needs and shop around for the best policies.**

or are self-employed, you may be able to purchase insurance through a professional association or group for small business owners. Many of these groups require you to become a member, but the price you'll pay for dues is minimal compared to what you'd pay for health care on your own.

An increasing number of people are choosing to join nonprofit insurance groups because they often promise large memberships and big discounts, and will lobby on behalf of members. But be cautious and do your research when buying these plans, because some of them may offer low teaser rates that are increased after a customer has signed up. In some cases, these groups may simply be a marketing tool for an insurance company or agents who buy their own associations and make them appear to be nonprofit groups.[2]

When you sign up for insurance, you'll pay a premium for the policy. Health maintenance organizations (HMOs) and preferred provider organizations (PPOs) offer an approved network of medical personnel that their customers can use. Both provide coverage for inpatient services such as hospital stays and outpatient services such as doctor's visits and prescriptions. The big difference between the plans is that PPOs may cover part of the costs of doctors who aren't in their approved network, while HMOs generally don't. Both plans usually require patients to make a fixed co-payment for visits to the doctor and for prescriptions.

Open access plans, which tend to be more expensive, give patients more flexibility because they can choose any doctor or hospital. The patient must pay a deductible up to a specific amount before the health plan begins to cover medical bills. After that, the plan may require a co-pay that is a certain percentage of the total bill for services. Because of the costs of such plans, they're usually too expensive for the average person to obtain on their own.

Thoroughly research any insurance plan you're considering so that you know you'll have access to the services and doctors you need and are confident that it's offered by a reputable provider. Many web sites offer insurance products that allow you to compare different plans and get actual quotes for some of them, but keep a healthy dose of skepticism. Plans that seem super cheap and require no medical information need further investigation. Also, celebrity endorsement does not guarantee a quality policy.

When using an agent, make sure that person is selling a state-licensed product. If they say they don't need a license because the coverage isn't insurance, is exempt from regulations, or is a union plan, avoid it. Union plans are set up by an employer or union for specific workers and aren't sold by insurance agents. If you aren't sure about a policy, you can always contact your state insurance department. The National Association of Insurance Commissioners web site at www.naic.org has links to the various state departments.

A Matter of Life and Death

If you have dependents, a life insurance policy is a must no matter what your marital status. Many employers offer life insurance policies at little or no cost to their employees. If you aren't sure whether your employer offers such a plan, check with your employee benefits department. Be sure to record the amount of any policies and the company contact information and keep it with important paperwork. If you're self-employed or unemployed, you'll need to shop around for a policy. You'll pay a fee for using an agent, but you'll be able to get your questions answered.

If an agent can't or won't explain a policy she's trying to sell you, then look for an agent who will. Why trust someone who isn't able or willing to take the time to help you make informed choices? "Counsel and sound judgment are mine; I have understanding and power" (Prov. 8:14).

Generally a policy covering five to seven times your annual income is sufficient, but you may need up to ten times your income if you have a lot of debt and financial obligations such as educational costs for your dependents. If you're a stay-at-home parent and don't earn any income, it's still important to be insured to cover any child care costs that might be necessary in the event of your death. So talk to your spouse to make sure you're both adequately covered. You don't need to purchase life insurance for minor children unless you rely upon income they earn.

To receive a price quote, you may be asked for some basic information, including your weight and whether you smoke. The cost of life insurance is based in large part on actuary tables that project life expectancy based on age, gender, and health. The purpose of these tables is to decide how much risk a potential customer is to an insurer. If you're obese, have poor health, or have a dangerous occupation, you're going to pay a higher premium.

Term life insurance is usually the least expensive type of coverage. You pay a fixed premium for a specific period of time, and if you die a death benefit is paid to your beneficiary. As you age or develop more health problems the premium may increase, but it's unlikely you'll pay as much as with a whole life policy. Whole life insurance applies the premium to a death benefit and to a savings or investment account inside the policy. These plans are usually a lot more expensive, and if you take money out of them, the amount of the death benefit is reduced. If you have other investments, generally it doesn't make sense to use insurance as an investment tool.

Save on Car Insurance

If you drive a car, then you probably have some type of insurance since many states require at least liability coverage, which pays for damage to other people and their property. Collision coverage is for damage to your vehicle if you have an accident, and comprehensive coverage deals with vandalism or natural events such as storms. All three types of coverage are usually required if you're still paying on a car loan or leasing.

The amount of the premium depends on which state the policy is written in as well as the driver's record. The average cost of auto insurance was $863 in 2005, and was expected to increase to $867 in 2006.[3]

Even if you already have a policy, it's worth shopping around to see if there are ways to lower the cost of insuring your vehicle. Inquire about any discounts that apply for having more than one type of policy with the same insurer. And if you use your car for business purposes, you should discuss this with your agent to make sure you're adequately covered.

If you file a claim, you'll pay a deductible for any necessary repairs. Many policies start out with a $250 deductible, but if you increase it to $500 or even $1,000 you can reduce the amount of your premium quite a bit. However, keep in mind that if you have an accident and need repairs on the car, you'll have to come up with the amount of the deductible. So be realistic about what you can afford when choosing to increase it.

In situations where a car is totaled, the insurer will write a check for the book value of the car, which might not be as high as you anticipate. If you drive an older car that no longer has a car note, you may decide that you only need liability coverage. But again, be prepared to pay out of your own pocket for any damage that occurs, and work to build a savings to cover such emergencies.

Getting airbags, automatic seatbelts, and anti-theft devices such as alarms can help lower premiums. Also, being a customer with the same insurer for many years or having multiple policies may reduce premiums, so ask your agent if you're eligible for this discount. If you have a teen driver in the house, showing that they have good grades or have taken a driver's education course may help reduce the cost.

For many people the type of car they drive is a status symbol. Not only do they pay $30,000 or more to have a prestigious car, but they spend more for insurance. Avoiding expensive sports cars or luxury vehicles not only will save you money on insurance, but will keep you from spending so many of your hard-earned dollars on a lease or loan. Is it really worth the cost to say you drive a Mercedes or BMW when you can't even save for your child's education or afford a down payment on that condo you've wanted to purchase?

Home Matters

The next area that most people need to address is insuring their home and belongings. If you're currently paying on a mortgage, then you should already have insurance. The price of the policy is based on several things, including the type of building, its age, and whether or not it's also used for business purposes. Prices vary with different insurers, so review your policy every couple of years to see if you're getting the best deal. Depending on the policy you have, your home will be insured against certain perils that are named in the contract. The more perils named, the higher your premium.

As with the other forms of insurance discussed, increasing your deductible will lower your premium. Check to see if your insurer offers discounts for installing security alarms and sprinkler systems, dead-bolt locks, and fire extinguishers. In some states, you may be eligible for a discount if you install hurricane/storm shutters and hurricane-resistant laminated glass windows and doors. Depending on where you live, you may need additional policies such as flood or earthquake insurance.

So how much insurance do you need? Insure at least 80 percent of the value of your home and the land it's on. When insuring your possessions, you want to look at the actual cash value versus the replacement cost. With actual cash value coverage you'll be reimbursed for the value of the property at the time of the claim minus the deductible, meaning items that depreciate won't get as large of a reimbursement as what you originally paid for them. So if you paid $1,000 for your big-screen TV four years ago, don't expect that much for it if you file a claim.

Replacement cost coverage reimburses the full value of possessions. If you have expensive items such as antiques or jewelry, you may want to purchase extra protection. Get in the habit of keeping receipts for major purchases in a safe place so that you'll have a record of their value if you do need to file an insurance claim. Day 23 discusses taking a home inventory. If you rent your home, you should look at policies that will insure your possessions against fire, theft, and other events. You don't have to insure the actual building because that's your landlord's responsibility.

These are the main types of insurance that most people have to consider at some point. Depending on your situation, you may want to decide whether you need disability insurance for if you're unable to work due to injury or illness. Many people buy disability policies because they are single and have no other source of income, or because they don't want family members to face financial hardship caring for them if they become incapacitated. These policies can be pretty expensive, so it's important to closely examine your situation to determine if it's a necessary expense.

Prayer Box

Lord, please bless me and my family and provide for our needs. I thank you for giving me options to provide for the future. Help me to sort through all of the various insurance policies and determine which ones are relevant to my situation. I understand the importance of not putting off these decisions and will be disciplined about making them. Amen.

A Place
to Call Home

My people will live in peaceful dwelling places, in secure homes, in undisturbed places of rest.

Isaiah 32:18

When I decided to buy a home in a suburban community several years ago, several people who knew me thought I was crazy. I wasn't married, had a nice apartment in New York, and didn't really know anyone in the burbs. And even if I bought a home, I was told I should just get a condo or co-op and not deal with all the upkeep. "Who's going to cut the grass and shovel the snow?" several people asked. "You'll never meet guys to date out there or have much social life," others lamented, sadly shaking their heads. "Isn't that a community with a bunch of families?" one woman whispered, as if *family* was a dirty word.

Despite my assurances to these people that I was eager to own my own home in a quiet, stable community, I'm sure

161

> **List goals for homeownership. Understand your motives for purchasing a home. Decide how much house you can afford and get your finances in order.**

many of them were still convinced I was making a bad choice. After all, aren't women supposed to wait for a husband to come along before getting into this whole business of buying property? If a woman buys a house, who's going to fix things if they break?

Because I had faith that I could handle the responsibility of a home, I took these comments in stride. Not only did I buy a house that came with a small yard, but I got myself some tools and learned how to make basic repairs. It took some adjusting to being in charge of a whole house and maintaining it properly, but buying it was one of the smartest financial moves I've ever made. And the best thing that came out of relocating to the supposedly social-life-challenged burbs? Meeting the wonderful man I now call my husband.

I didn't realize it at the time, but when I bought that house in the mid '90s I was part of a growing trend of single women becoming first-time homeowners. About 53 percent of female-headed households owned homes in 2000, up from 48 percent in the early 1980s, according to the Joint Center for Housing Studies at Harvard University. The number of women under 45 who where first-time home buyers and lived alone rose 65 percent between 1985 and 1999. By 2010, Fannie Mae expects that about 31 million single women, or 28 percent of all U.S. households, will own homes. Not only are many women (like men) tired of renting year after year without building any equity, but they've been able to take advantage of lower interest rates and less stringent requirements for down payments.

Maybe you've been dreaming of owning your own home for years. Or perhaps you've bought into the idea that a single woman doesn't really need a house. If you are planning to buy, have you done your homework to figure out if you qualify for a mortgage? If you're married, have you discussed your hopes for buying a home with your spouse and come to an agreement on what this means for your family's finances? If you're single, are you really ready to commit to all the responsibility and upkeep that come with a home?

Your Dream Home

Write your goals for home ownership in your journal. Even if you're not a first-time homebuyer but intend to purchase another home, this section will help plan for that event. In your goal statement, focus on what characteristics you're looking for in a home and community. Are you looking for good schools, plenty of outdoor recreation, community involvement opportunities, or low crime rates? Do you have a growing family and need plenty of bedrooms, bathrooms, and outdoor space? Is a home office important because you telecommute or operate a home business?

Make a note of which characteristics are absolutely necessary, such as a large kitchen or a playroom for your kids. Next, decide which items are negotiable, such as a fireplace or a swimming pool. Any characteristics left on the list are probably things you would like to have but can live without. Know the difference between what's necessary and what's not before you begin your house hunt. "The wise woman builds her house, but with her own hands the foolish one tears hers down" (Prov. 14:1).

Look at your list again. Is it based on things you really don't need but are hoping will impress relatives and friends?

163

Do you really need twenty-foot ceilings and a *Gone with the Wind* staircase? Be honest about whether you're being too materialistic and trying to keep up certain appearances. Are you being unrealistic by wanting a swimming pool in the backyard when you know you really can't afford the maintenance and upkeep? It's one thing to enjoy such luxuries when you have the money to pay for them, but it's another to go broke trying to live up to a certain lavish lifestyle.

If you're more concerned with imitating *Lifestyles of the Rich and Famous* than with providing a stable, comfortable home for you and your family, then maybe your priorities are mixed up. If you feel deep inside that this is true, then ask God to help you focus on what's really important and to diminish your appetite for so many material things. Think about why it's more important to have a home be a retreat and a haven than to have it be a showplace for the world. Try not to focus on having the biggest, most expensively decorated home because you're trying to outdo friends and neighbors. No matter how much money you spend on keeping up the "right" appearance, there's always going to be someone with more money and a bigger, fancier house. "Whoever loves money never has money enough; whoever loves wealth is never satisfied with his income. This too is meaningless" (Eccles. 5:10).

Next, examine your finances to determine if you're really ready to purchase a home. Have you ordered your credit report and corrected any mistakes? Have you gone through your monthly bills and statements so that you know how much of your income is needed for these items? Did you add up the amount of any debts you may owe? Do you know how much of your savings you can allocate toward a down payment? Do you even have a savings account to tap for this purpose? If you haven't done any of these necessary steps, then go back and take care of them before going any further with trying to purchase a home. Not only do you need to understand your whole financial picture, but if you intend to get a mortgage, lenders will ask for the same information.

When deciding if you're a good risk for a mortgage, one of the main things a lender will look at is the ratio of your income for monthly housing payments and debts. The most common ratio for conventional loans is 28/36, with the first number being the percentage of your gross income that you should spend on housing (including insurance and property taxes) and the second number being the percentage of all your debt, including housing. This ratio may differ somewhat, depending on the lender, how much cash you have for a down payment, and whether or not it's a Federal Housing Authority (FHA) loan.

Qualifying for a Mortgage

Refer to the worksheet in figure 21.1 to calculate your maximum mortgage payment for housing and debt ratio. Multiply your total income—including salary, child support, and any other sources—by .28, then divide by 12 to determine the maximum you should spend on housing each month. Next, multiply your income by .36, then divide by 12 to determine the total amount of debt, including housing, that you should pay each month. For example, if you have an annual income of $65,000, you shouldn't pay more than $1,516 a month for housing and $1,950 for total debt. Keep your mortgage-debt ratio in mind as you begin to look at homes and shop for a lender.

Maximum Mortgage Payment Ratio

Gross Income_____× .28_____
        ÷ 12
Maximum Monthly Mortgage Payment_____

Maximum Debt Ratio

Gross Income_____× .36_____
        ÷ 12
Maximum Monthly Debt_____

Figure 21.1

When you're serious about buying, you should begin by looking at different lending institutions and comparing interest rates. If you're working with an experienced realtor, she should be able to suggest which lenders in your area have the best rates, but interview at least three lenders before choosing one. If you choose to use a mortgage broker, they'll charge a fee to find a lender and handle the paperwork. That cost is on top of any application fee the lender charges.

Once you apply for a mortgage, you'll be asked to verify your income with paycheck stubs and/or income tax returns. The lender will also want verification that you have a 5 percent to 20 percent down payment, which can come from your own bank accounts or be given as a gift by a family member. Check with your lender about loans insured through the Federal Housing Administration (FHA) or guaranteed by the Department of Veterans Affairs. The advantage to these programs is they often require smaller down payments.

Remember, the lower the down payment, the higher the monthly mortgage payment since there will be more principal to pay. Putting down less than 20 percent usually requires the purchase of Private Mortgage Insurance (PMI), in case a homebuyer defaults on a loan. Once there's equity in the home of 20 percent, the bank may or may not cancel PMI, so ask the lender about its policy. Decide whether it makes sense to wait a little longer to save up more for the down payment or go with one of these lending plans.

You'll also be asked whether you want a fixed-rate mortgage, which has the same interest payments throughout the term of the loan, or an adjustable rate, which can fluctuate over time. The length of the loan will affect how much interest is paid over the life of the loan. Some loans have short terms and a large final payment that's called a balloon. Sometimes borrowers pay points to get a better interest rate, with each point equaling 1 percent of the amount of the loan. Points are usually tax deductible, so talk with your tax advisor or lender about your situation.

Other closing costs may include the application fee, property appraisals, credit reports, title, and attorneys fees. The loan paperwork will include the Truth in Lending Disclosure Statement that will show you the loan's payment information and include the APR, which includes interest, points, and certain other fees.

Besides paying principal and interest, you'll have to get homeowner's insurance and, depending on where you live, possibly insurance for floods or other natural disasters. These extra insurance policies can add significantly to your monthly payments and may even cost more than the main homeowner's policy. Property taxes will also have to be paid and will vary depending on where you live. Insurance and taxes can be paid separately or wrapped into your mortgage payments and put into an escrow account, which is set up to guarantee that you pay these fees on time. As you can see, all of these fees increase the amount of your monthly housing costs beyond the original mortgage.

If you need more information on buying a home, visit the Department of Housing and Urban Affairs web site at www.hud.gov.

Prayer Box

Lord, please help me to keep my priorities straight for owning and maintaining a home. I want my home to be a haven and retreat. Please help me not to focus on unnecessary characteristics just to impress other people. I realize that having the biggest, most expensive house isn't as important as finding a place that meets my needs (and those of my family). I know that you will continue to provide for me and that I don't have to worry about having my needs met. Amen.

Plan Your Estate

I was young and now I am old, yet I have never seen the
righteous forsaken or their children begging bread. They
are always generous and lend freely; their children will
be blessed.

Psalm 37:25–26

Some people say the world is going to the dogs. In the
case of one California woman, that was pretty much
true. When Marie Dana's boyfriend of six years, Sid-
ney Altman, died, she expected to inherit his nearly $6 mil-
lion estate. But she was stunned to learn that the bulk of
the inheritance was left to the man's cocker spaniel. Dana
was named as the dog's legal guardian and given a $60,000
a year stipend. She was also to have full use of Altman's
Beverly Hills home until the dog's death, at which time his
estate would pass to two animal rights charities.[1]

In Australia, socialite Rose Porteous said she was leaving $1 million to each of her two poodles, whom she de-
scribed as her best friends. Porteous said she had written

> **Form an estate plan to provide for your family's needs in the event of your death or other emergency. Choose appropriate estate planning documents for your situation.**

her dogs, Dennis and Lulu, into her will after going through a bitter court fight over $20 million left by her late husband. She wanted to make sure the dogs, whom she spent most of her time with, would be provided for and said she didn't want to take any chances of that not happening. She stipulated that after the dogs died the rest of their inheritance would go to a rescue center for poodles.[2]

As unbelievable as these stories sound, they're true. And they illustrate a pretty simple point about estate planning: You've got to have a plan in order to make your wishes known after you die, even if they do appear ridiculous or unfair to your survivors. Porteous explained her actions, but who knows what Altman was thinking when he wrote his will, or how he really felt about his girlfriend. One thing we can surmise from this story is that he loved his dog a lot!

How much do you love your family? Do you love them enough to plan ahead for their future in case you die unexpectedly? Most of us would answer an emphatic yes to that question, yet many Americans don't even have a basic will.

Facing a Difficult Task

Facing death isn't an easy task for many people. It's hard thinking about losing loved ones or not fulfilling lifelong dreams. Many people fear death so much that they won't allow themselves to think about leaving life on earth. This fear and avoidance may even cause them—consciously or unconsciously—to put off forming an estate plan. But having such a blueprint can help ensure that family members are provided for after a person dies. And while many single people with few assets may not really need a will, that changes as their net worth increases.

Have you thought about what will happen to your belongings after you're gone? The process of estate planning isn't meant to be an exercise in hoarding possessions or micromanaging what happens to them. Instead, it's simply making sure that assets are distributed to the people you want to have them as well as settling unfinished business. If you have minor children, planning ahead can ensure that they are cared for according to your wishes.

A will is a written document that states who should inherit your property and care for minor children. Without a will, a person is declared intestate, meaning the state decides who receives the assets and cares for any children. So if you want your sister to have your great-aunt Millie's antique china, you need to make that known in a will. If you're married, have separate wills drawn up for you and your spouse, even if you're leaving everything to each other. Joint wills can complicate things and tie up property for years.

If you're a parent and don't want a stranger who knows nothing about your situation to decide who will care for your children, then having a will is a necessity, not an option. This is true whether you're single or married. Choosing a guardian for your children in the event of your death (or you and your spouse) is a major decision. Decide who you trust with the care and upbringing of your children and ask them if they are willing to accept that responsibility before naming them in your will.

Hollywood has made numerous films about the unsuspecting single person with the "perfect life" suddenly being informed that they've been chosen as the guardian for a relative's children. These shell-shocked people whine and protest, then reluctantly take in the orphans (who are usually cute and precocious). Halfway through the film, the guardian quickly changes from being grumpy and resentful to completely doting on the children. In real life, skip the drama of the surprise announcement, and make sure you choose someone who truly is willing to see your kids to adulthood and beyond.

If your financial situation isn't very complicated, you may be able to write the will yourself using forms from a stationery store or legal software. Should you decide to go the do-it-yourself route, I suggest using the software, which will walk you through the process. Once the document is complete, you may want to have your attorney review it. To make it legal the will must be dated and signed in front of at least two witnesses, depending on your state of residence.

The Probate Process

A lot of people mistakenly believe that if they have a will their estate doesn't go through probate, but that isn't true. Probate is simply the legal process of determining that a will is valid, inventorying and disposing of assets, and paying debts after a person dies. Legal and court fees are paid out of the estate. An executor, either named by the deceased or appointed by the court, files the paperwork and is responsible for overseeing the process. Any adult, including an attorney, can serve as an executor. Many singles choose a parent or sibling to act as their executor, while married folks often choose their spouse. If you want to name an executor, pick someone who is trustworthy and has good judgment.

Probate can be avoided by creating a living trust, which is a document that gives legal title for your property to an individual, called a trustee, while you're still alive. After your death, property in the trust would be transferred to your beneficiaries. Once all of the property is transferred the trust will no longer exist.

Unlike wills, which become public records when filed at probate court, living trusts never have to be made public. If you aren't sure of what to put in a trust or will, or if you have a large estate, you're probably better off paying an attorney to do it for you. Also, if you write a living trust, you should still have a will to cover any belongings that haven't been transferred to the trust because they were acquired after it was formed.

Unless you have an estate valued at $1 million or more as of 2003, you won't have to worry about paying estate tax. Only about 2 percent of all estates are required to pay estate tax, according to the IRS. The estate tax exemption is scheduled to increase to $3.5 million in 2009 and to be repealed in 2010. If you have a large estate that you expect to be taxed after your death, you can take advantage of the $1 million lifetime gift tax exemption. This exemption allows you to make a total of $1 million of taxable gifts over your lifetime before owing a federal gift tax. While saving money on taxes shouldn't be the primary motive for giving, this strategy does have benefits to people with high net worth. If you'd like to know more about estate taxes, contact a tax attorney or accountant to discuss your situation.

Many people are satisfied with having only a will. However, in addition to designating who should receive personal property, estate planning can also include a healthcare directive, which addresses what type of medical care a person wants if they become seriously ill or incapacitated. A declaration is a document written directly to medical personnel about what types of care are acceptable and unacceptable. A durable power of attorney for healthcare appoints another individual to make decisions about your care if you can't do it yourself. These documents must be signed in front of witnesses or a notary public, depending on where you live. You can also write a durable power of attorney to have your financial affairs handled.

As with choosing guardians for children, appointing an agent for your healthcare or financial decisions is a serious step. If you have certain spiritual or moral beliefs, you'll want the person you choose to share them or at least be willing to respect and honor them. Pray over this matter and really think about who you would trust with your life. If you're married, you'll probably name your spouse. Single women may choose to name a parent, sibling, or close friend but should avoid naming a boyfriend with whom they don't have a secure future.

Having an accident or major illness occur can sometimes bring out the worst in family members who may be stressed, upset, and argumentative over who should make major medical and financial decisions for an incapacitated person. I've witnessed situations where spouses of seriously ill individuals were bullied and manipulated by other family members who wanted to be in charge of all decision making. Deciding ahead of time who will make important decisions for you can help avoid some of this wrangling.

To find an attorney to help plan your estate, ask family and friends if they can recommend someone they trust. Before you meet with a lawyer, be prepared with the names and contact information of the people you plan to leave property to. Copies of estate planning documents can be kept on file in the attorney's office, but you should also keep a copy at home in a place where it can be found if anything happens to you. If you write your own will, you can file it with an attorney or leave the original in a safe-deposit box and keep a copy at home with the key.

If you're like I was when I first sat down to write a will, you may be thinking, "What do I have that's even worth giving to anyone?" Well, you may be surprised after taking an inventory of your possessions at how many things actually have great sentimental value and would be enjoyed by other family members. In some instances, you'll realize there are things sitting around the house that may actually have some monetary value. The next day of your makeover will help you take an inventory of your home to help with estate planning and documenting belongings for insurance purposes.

Prayer Box

Dear Lord, I know that my time on this earth is not permanent and that I will find eternal life in heaven with you. Help me to have the character of a good steward and not be reluctant or fearful about estate planning. I want to make good decisions and inform my loved ones of my wishes in the event that I am no longer able to do so. Thank you for helping me to face these decisions and not avoid them. Amen.

Home Inventory

In the house of the wise are stores of choice food and oil,
but a foolish man devours all he has.

Proverbs 21:20

f you had an earthquake, fire, or burglary at your home,
would you be able to remember all of your belongings
and their approximate value? Would you know how to
positively identify stolen items that later turned up at a
local police department? In 2003, there were 388,500 home
fires in the U.S., resulting in $5.9 billion in direct property
damage.[1] And over 6 million burglaries, or one every ten
seconds, occur each year in American homes.[2]

While many people have homeowner's or renter's insurance and assume that all their losses will be covered in an
emergency, that isn't necessarily true. Insurers will work to
resolve any claims filed, but it's ultimately your responsibility to prove those losses. For example, if you have a homeowner's policy that covers $75,000 for personal property,
that's the maximum amount you would be paid to replace
all of your household belongings. That personal property

would include clothing, furniture, toys, artwork, appliances, and so forth. If you have very expensive items and feel that your existing personal property insurance is inadequate for all of your belongings, talk with your insurer to add additional coverage.

> **Document and photograph your belongings for insurance and estate planning. Store your inventory in an off-site location.**

To document belongings, take an inventory of your home and photograph it. This will help place a value on household items for future reference. An inventory is helpful not only when deciding how much insurance to carry and when filing claims, but also when writing estate-planning documents. With this list, you can tell your insurer how much your set of antique silver is worth if it's stolen in a burglary, and you'll also have a picture of it for your brother in Idaho if you choose to leave it to him in your will. Both homeowners and renters should do a home inventory.

Protect Your Inventory

This task can be completed in a couple of hours and requires use of a camera. You can also use a video camera to back up photos. Once you've completed the inventory, get two sets of prints. One should be kept at home in a fireproof box and the other should be kept with a relative or friend who doesn't live near you, since a fire or natural disaster could destroy a close neighbor's home, too. You can also keep a copy of the prints in a safe-deposit box. Some insurers provide home inventory books where you can store your photographs and receipts, so be sure to ask your agent about this.

While there are many companies offering home inventory services and software, why pay someone else to do what you can accomplish in a short time with little cost? Just copy the worksheet in figure 23.1 to record information and keep with your photos.

Home Inventory

Item	Serial number	Value	Extra insurance / Warranty

Figure 23.1

When photographing your home, make sure you have adequate light. Open the curtains to let in light and be sure your camera has a working flash. Higher speed film such as 400 or 800 can help to get better shots in dark closets and hallways. If you're using a digital camera and plan to store photos on a computer or a disk, you'll still need to make prints that can be kept in a safe place outside your home.

Consider Extra Insurance

Start at the bottom of your home and work your way up. Take a picture of all walls in order to get an overall view of the contents. If you have valuable items such as jewelry, rare books, or antiques, take close-up shots that show the detail and any identifying marks. Have these belongings appraised since assigning a fair market value to items without identifying marks can be very subjective. Don't forget the china, silver service, or fur that may be in storage.

As you go through each room, write down a brief description of major belongings on the home inventory sheet. If there are model and serial numbers, such as on electronics, write that next to the description. If you know the purchase price, you can put that in the last column. But remember, if you file a claim, you probably won't receive that full amount because of depreciation, so don't expect your twenty-year-old La-Z-Boy recliner that your cat uses as a scratching post to fetch what you originally paid for it.

As you go through the kitchen, bedrooms, and hallways, open all closets and cabinets and photograph the contents. Don't forget to document the contents of your basement and attic and any additional storage sheds. If you have recreational vehicles, bicycles, or tools, record the serial numbers and other identifying information. I regularly scan the police blotter reports in my local newspaper and am sometimes amazed at the brazenness of thieves who walk into people's yards in broad daylight to steal lawn equipment, ladders, grills, and anything else sitting around.

Be sure to get photos of the outside of all buildings on your property, including barns and detached garages. Take several pictures from different sides of the buildings. Don't forget photos of swimming pools, expensive landscaping, and fences. Also, get several shots of your car, boat, or motorcycle from different angles in case they're stolen and have to be traced.

Once you develop your prints, write serial numbers, brands, markings, or artists' names on the back with a permanent marker. You also may want to store the negatives at the off-site location. If you have receipts for your most recent purchases or certificates of authenticity for collectibles, make copies and include them in your inventory.

The purpose of gathering all this information is to protect you and your family. By setting up a system of documentation, you can be sure to have adequate insurance and access to important information you may need in an emergency. While a theft or catastrophic loss can be difficult to deal with, having a home inventory stored in a safe location can help alleviate some of the stress and confusion that may arise.

Prayer Box

Lord, thank you for my home and belongings. Help me to be better organized and to care for them in the appropriate manner. I know that it is important to be responsible and plan ahead for the future, and having a home inventory will help me in this area. I don't want to document my household out of fear or greed, but because I want to be a good caretaker of what you've given me. Please remind me of items that should be included. Amen.

Stick to a Budget

I can do everything through him who gives me strength.

Philippians 4:13

Probably one of the least enjoyable tasks for many people when organizing their finances is setting up and following a budget. It's not the actual process of deciding how much money to spend in certain categories that gets to most people. It's being disciplined enough to not spend more than allocated in each area.

While setting strict limits on spending may seem like a burden, in the long run it will help you prioritize purchases and trim the fat. After all, how many pairs of shoes and matching handbags does one woman need? And does it really make sense to buy expensive jewelry or designer nails when the rent has to be paid? Many women who are addicted to shopping can tell stories of how they have brand-new clothing with the tags still attached that they've never worn and may not even be able to fit into. Don't set yourself

> **Set up a monthly budget. Determine if you're living above your means and find ways to cut spending. Seek help if your financial behavior is more than you can handle alone.**

up for failure by not having a blueprint to follow with your purchases.

I used to find budgeting to be a useless chore because I never followed my own guidelines and would quickly become discouraged. I'd stare in disbelief at my empty wallet and shrinking checking account balance and wrack my brain to remember where I'd spent my money. What got me were the miscellaneous purchases made with money withdrawn from ATMs, not the recurring bills such as rent or utilities. But after making a conscious effort to stick to the amounts budgeted and keep track of receipts, I began to see changes in how much money I had in my bank account at the end of each month. Using the budget-planning tool on my Quicken program—something I highly recommend if you have a computer—helped me to further organize and dissect my spending habits by categories.

Set Realistic Goals

Use the information compiled as you worked through this book to set up a budget. I've chosen to save this step for near the end of your 25-day makeover so you'll already have a complete picture of your spending, debt, savings, and other financial obligations.

Hopefully by now you've thought about ways to trim spending in certain areas and to put more toward tithing and saving. The goal for budgeting is to set realistic spending amounts, not lofty ones that only look good on paper but are impossible to implement. If you've done the exercises in the preceding chapters, you should have all the information you need to set up a budget that works for your situation.

Once you draw up this guide, keep it in a place where you can refer to it regularly to make sure you're on track. Stick it on a bulletin board or refrigerator if that helps. If you're using financial software to do this, set up the alert feature that lets you know when your spending in each category has surpassed the limit.

Add up your total monthly income, including paychecks, child support, or social security, and enter it in the chart in figure 24.1 on the following page. Then list your actual monthly spending in each of the areas that apply to your situation. If your expenses in certain areas fluctuate from month to month, use an average dollar figure. To do this, go back through your checkbook and add up the totals in a category for the last six months, then divide by six. You should be able to transfer most of the information for your budget from your checkbook and expense tracker. Don't forget to include expenses that you pay quarterly or annually, such as insurance premiums, dues, or home security fees.

If your expenses total more than your income, you're living above your means and need to put the brakes on your spending *now*. If your income is equal to or higher than expenses, there may still be areas where you can save money. Just because you make a certain amount of money doesn't mean you have to spend it all.

Look at each category and decide if you can cut spending there. Write down the most you plan to spend in that category in the budgeted column. This is now the maximum amount you should spend in each area over a month's time. Obviously you won't be able to change fixed amounts such as a mortgage or car payment (unless you refinance), but you may be able to cut spending in areas such as cable TV, long distance phone calls, or personal grooming.

Budget

	Actual	Budgeted	Difference
Income			
Salary			
Child support			
Social security			
Other income			
Total income			
Expenses			
Mortgage			
Household			
Home repair			
Utilities			
Home security			
Trash removal			
Groceries			
Dining out			
Personal care			
Memberships			
Hobbies			
Recreation			
Entertainment			
Travel			
Gifts			
Education			
Medical			

	Actual	Budgeted	Difference
Insurance			
Auto			
Credit cards			
Other loans			
Savings			
Retirement			
Investments			
Subscriptions			
Other			
Other			
Total expenses			

Total income - Total expenses = _____*

*A negative surplus means you are living above your means!

Figure 24.1

Be honest with yourself about whether overspending in certain areas is a drag on your overall fiscal health. Perhaps you've been paying monthly dues for membership at a health club that you haven't visited in months. (Been there, done that.) Or maybe your family goes to the movies every weekend and buys the expensive snacks when you could choose to rent movies more often at your local public library or video store. What about unhealthy habits you support such as buying fast food every night or smoking? Once you decide on areas to cut back, remind yourself that you're more than a conqueror and can achieve your goals (Rom. 8:37).

We live in a society where instant gratification is encouraged and those who deny themselves certain luxuries such as cable TV are laughed at or regarded as odd. Instead of saving up to make a major purchase, we're encouraged to "buy it now" on credit without considering how we'll pay for it when we get the bill. Like cartoon characters Wilma Flintstone and Betty Rubble, many of us hear about a sale and rush out to the mall with credit cards in hand yelling "Charge it!" without any self-control.

The Overall Picture

Stop and think about whether or not there are areas of your life that are out of control. If your finances are in chaos, then other areas of your life probably are, too. How's your physical health? Do you have stomachaches or feel stressed or panicked, particularly when thinking about money? Are you feeling spiritually disconnected because no matter what you do you just can't seem to get ahead and don't believe you can rely on God? Maybe you got laid off from your job and can't sleep for wondering why it happened to you and what the next move should be. Are your emotions frequently on edge, resulting in crying fits or angry outbursts directed at family and friends?

If you're married, do you and your husband frequently fight about money issues and have trouble agreeing on major decisions? Do you constantly engage in negative self-talk, telling yourself that you're stupid, useless, or will never amount to much? As a result, have you told yourself not to even bother reining in your out-of-control spending and other behaviors?

"Shame and self-talk are the two things that probably prevent us from choosing godly behavior and accepting that we're truly loved and redeemed," says counselor Trudy Colflesh. "Self-talk of a poverty spirit is 'I'm helpless. Nothing good happens to me. I get all the bad breaks. I'm less than other people.'" The more a person feels this way and gets depressed over their circumstances, the less energy they'll have to try and change things, says Colflesh. They may even begin to engage in fantasies about winning lotteries or coming into a financial windfall to solve all their problems. But there is no quick fix to solving issues. Instead of praying for everything to change overnight, it's more realistic to slowly implement changes that can be added to like building blocks. Reviewing your finances and making a budget are good starting points to improving your financial habits.

If your problems are too much to handle alone, seek the help of a minister, counselor, or support group that can keep you accountable in a caring atmosphere. "God wants us to realize we're loved. A lot of people have to feel they're loved by humans before they'll understand God loves them," says Colflesh. "But it doesn't surprise God that you're in this situation . . . He doesn't have an unrealistic expectation of you and your circumstances, but God doesn't want you to have to live in this misery."

Perhaps your situation isn't serious enough for counseling and you just need to take time out to check your behavior and refocus your priorities. Even if your day is jam-packed with work, activities, and other obligations, find just fifteen minutes to stop what you're doing and relax. Go into your bedroom, bathroom, car—anywhere you can be alone without being interrupted by children or phones—and close your eyes and breathe deeply. Feel God's presence around you and remember that he will always be with you, no matter how difficult things get.

It's easy to sing the Lord's praises when we're flush with cash and feel on top of the world. But a true test of faith is believing that we're blessed and will continue to be even when we're down to our last dollar and a week away from payday. "Now faith is being sure of what we hope for and certain of what we do not see" (Heb. 11:1).

Don't get bogged down in what has happened in the past. Make a decision today to change just one negative behavior that's keeping you from being fiscally fit. Ask the Lord to give you strength and courage to face this area. Work on conquering that issue and then move on to the next one.

Single ladies, don't feel you have to do this alone. Find an accountability partner (not a man) or a singles group with whom you can talk openly. If you have friction in your marriage over money, ask your husband to pray with you and work through your issues together in a loving fashion. Perhaps joining a group with other couples will help you have open and honest dialogue without escalating into shouting matches. After all, you're in this together, not playing on opposite teams. Even if you have to work through a lot of personal stuff before you can begin implementing steps such as writing a budget, you're going to make progress if you acknowledge your shortcomings and make a decision to fix them.

Prayer Box

Lord, thank you for your love and grace. I believe in the ability to change my life by putting all my trust in you. Help me to break old patterns of negative behavior and become a new creature in you. I understand that budgeting my money and being disciplined in this area will help me be a better manager of my finances overall. This may mean denying myself certain luxuries, but I'm willing to do this to get my financial house in order. Amen.

Shop Smarter

Free me from the trap that is set for me, for you are my
refuge. Into your hands I commit my spirit; redeem me,
O LORD, the God of truth.

Psalm 31:4–5

Making your money stretch further takes effort and
organization, but it isn't impossible. Maybe you're
not going to drive to five supermarkets just to get
the best deal on canned goods, or camp out at three in the
morning to be first in line at the store, but you want to
know how to shop smarter. In this era of warehouse stores,
outlet malls, and Internet auctions, there really is no reason
you have to pay the full retail price for many items. But
shopping smarter and saving money goes beyond finding
discount prices. It's important to understand your motiva-
tion for shopping and to have a strategy before you even
reach the store.

Think about what makes you tick when it comes to
spending money. Are you excited by the thrill of the hunt? Is

> **Determine what emotions may contribute to your spending behaviors. Evaluate how you feel when you shop. Plan goals for shopping trips before leaving home.**

shopping an escape from your obligations or problems going on in your life? Do you have issues with self-esteem and buy things that you believe will make you more attractive to others? Is shopping a way to show the world how much style and good taste you have?

Karen grew up in a poor family and wore a lot of secondhand clothing, some of which came from other kids at her school. "It was embarrassing to get a 'new' outfit out of a bag of hand-me-down clothes only to find out when you wear it to school that it used to belong to a classmate's sister," she says. As a young person Karen found an outlet for her feelings through her artwork. At sixteen she began working at a fast-food restaurant and earning her own money, so she began buying things for herself using layaway plans to satisfy her hunger for new and fashionable clothing. "It would take me two months to buy a pair of pants on layaway, and while I was at the store to pick them up, I would inevitably see something else I wanted and start a new layaway."

Once Karen got her own credit cards, her spending escalated as she bought things to reflect her likes, dislikes, and attitudes. Shopping became such a form of expression that it replaced her interest in drawing and writing. And as the credit card bills piled up she'd get depressed. "Then I would need new things to cheer me up. I would buy them, get more bills, and get more depressed."

Now 29, Karen says the realization that she and her husband are $74,000 in debt and can't afford to buy a home or travel has reined in her spending. "I have prayed for God . . . to help me be satisfied with what I have and help me find other ways to express myself," she says. "I still get a shopping bug every so often, but I haven't bought anything on credit in about eight months. My new policy is cash only and no layaway either!"

Women and Shopping

According to a study of gender differences in financial behavior, 36 percent of women versus 18 percent of men were more likely to buy something without needing it; 24 percent versus 5 percent said they can't resist a sale; and 31 percent versus 19 percent shop to celebrate.[1] Understanding your motivations for shopping will help you evaluate whether or not you need to make a purchase. "Now this is what the LORD Almighty says: 'Give careful thought to your ways. You have planted much, but have harvested little. You eat, but never have enough. You drink, but never have your fill. You put on clothes, but are not warm. You earn wages, only to put them in a purse with holes in it'" (Hag. 1:5–6).

For many women, shopping isn't really about getting something shiny and new, but is more about validating themselves and feeling good. "I've gone shopping because I felt blue, and getting out of the house and looking at different things helped in a way to get my mind off whatever was nagging at me," says Marianne, 24. "Those are the times I end up buying stuff I tell myself that I could use but I end up not really using them."

In many ways, society encourages women to spend more. Women often are responsible for buying necessities and other items for their family and home. Also, the media constantly bombards women with images of the latest fashions and accessories, leading them to believe they have to keep spending to stay current with trends or look like an out-of-style frump. Men don't have the same pressure to always be fashionable and can often get away with wearing the same suit for years without the fashion police pointing fingers. But honestly, how many pairs of Prada shoes do you need? And is a $30 lipstick really better than one that only costs $5?

Think about the last few times you went shopping, including at the supermarket and online. Write in your journal what you can recall about how you felt before you made your purchase. Were you going strictly because you had to stock up on food for your family? Or were you trying to get away from an abusive husband? Did you stick with what was on a list or pick up a lot of impulse items? Think about how you felt as you walked out of the store with your purchase and record that in your journal. Did you experience euphoria, a sense of accomplishment, or worry about getting the credit card bill?

Now write down feelings you may have had later that day or the next about your shopping trip. Were you satisfied you'd found the best deal, or remorseful or angry for buying what you really couldn't afford? Did you buy fattening snacks because you were upset over breaking up with your boyfriend? Perhaps you bought items you didn't need through a television shopping channel because you were bored and lonely.

Even if you can't remember how you felt the last time you made a purchase, begin recording your feelings the next time you shop. Doing this over a period of time will help detect patterns in behavior that you can then work to change. If part of what's fueling out-of-control spending and other negative behaviors is gambling, alcohol, or drug abuse, get help ASAP. Talk to your pastor or a counselor about getting into a treatment program to begin your healing. Ask trusted family and friends to pray for you and offer support.

Confronting the Truth

Self-discovery and self-realization can be awesome and liberating. They can also be uncomfortable and somewhat scary. After getting at the cause of harmful attitudes and behaviors, you may feel embarrassed and ashamed. But you're only human, and the Creator won't love you any less for making mistakes.

When Adam and Eve ate the fruit from the tree of knowledge and became aware of their nakedness, they were ashamed and tried to hide from God. They didn't understand that the Father had always known they were naked and imperfect but loved his children because they were his. Instead of beating up on yourself for what may have happened in the past, ask the Lord for forgiveness and the courage to break free of unhealthy habits. Read Psalm 32 for encouragement about confessing your sins and receiving mercy and deliverance.

If shopping with certain friends who encourage you to make unnecessary purchases has been part of the problem, then stop going with them. If it's impossible to completely avoid being around certain individuals, such as your sister or a cousin, then leave your checkbook and credit cards at home when you're out with them and carry only a small amount of cash. Ask them to support your efforts to change by not egging you on to spend money.

When you have to make purchases, compose a well thought-out list before you head out of your house. Plan your meals for the next week or two and buy only those groceries that you need. If you feel that you must have the most prestigious brands in expensive gourmet food stores, stop and think about what you hope to gain. Are those brands really higher in quality, or do you feel pressured to steer clear of items that your friends will view as lower class? Maybe you grew up on welfare or your parents always bought the cheapest store brands and now you feel you owe it to yourself to splurge on the pricey stuff.

If you're shopping for clothing, look in your closet to evaluate your current wardrobe. If you already have three navy skirts and six pairs of barely worn black shoes, why buy more? Write down items that you truly need and how much you can afford to spend (refer back to your budget). Buy classic, well-made styles that will outlast changing fashion trends. If you're fighting an addiction to shopping, only shop for items on your list and don't linger in stores (see figure 25.1).

Ten Ways to Cut Expenses

1. Buy used clothing for babies and small children or swap with other parents.
2. Pack a special homemade meal in a nice basket and have a romantic picnic in the park.
3. Put spare change in a jar at the end of each day. When it's filled up, deposit it in your savings account.
4. Borrow videos, DVDs, and CDs from the library.
5. Buy and sell old clothing at consignment shops.
6. Get rid of a gym membership if you never use it. Take long walks, invest in a piece of exercise equipment you'll use, or shoot hoops with your family.
7. Get a family plan for your cell phones.
8. Increase insurance deductibles.
9. Set a strict budget when planning your wedding and stick to it.
10. Get rid of magazine subscriptions you no longer read.

Figure 25.1

Find ways to socialize with your girlfriends other than going on shopping trips. Fill your time up with hobbies and activities that don't cost anything. Also, think about volunteering in your community. As you become involved with giving your time and attention to worthwhile causes and helping others, you won't have as much free time to devote to spending money. God has a purpose for your life greater than you may imagine (see Jer. 29:11).

If you're fighting an uphill battle against shopping and are at your wits end about what to do, consider joining a support group for people with out-of-control spending behaviors, such as Debtors Anonymous at www.debtorsanonymous. org (781-453-2743). These groups offer 12-step programs that incorporate things such as prayer, analyzing personal habits, and being accountable to peers when overcoming destructive habits. Perhaps your church has a financial ministry that helps people break free of such bondage and learn good financial habits. Every makeover has to start somewhere, so why not start by changing what's going on inside of you?

Prayer Box

Lord, help me to control my spending and not be controlled by the world's messages about what I should buy. Help me to keep my needs and wants in perspective so that I'm not just lusting after material possessions or coveting what my neighbor has. I don't want to spend all my free time shopping, and I know there is other, more important business I need to be about for my Father. Thank you for leading me on this 25-day journey into financial freedom and wholeness. Please continue to reveal to me ways I can remain committed to this journey I have begun. Show me how I can be an encouragement to others. Amen.

Conclusion

The 25-Day Money Makeover for Women is at an end, but your journey to establish better financial habits that will last a lifetime isn't over. Some of your goals and priorities may change or become more defined according to your situation. Refer to this book as often as necessary to redo some of the questions or exercises in areas that are pertinent. As you make progress toward becoming a better manager of your resources, you'll begin to see fruit in different areas of your life. While it may not always be easy to curb spending or other destructive habits that have been established over many years, just keep remembering that you are a child of God and can do all things through him.

I hope that you've been inspired to take authority over any areas of your financial life that have suffered or just need to be improved. If you're still seeking support for your journey, find a prayer partner or group with whom you can work through these issues. You don't have to struggle with this alone and may end up helping others in the process. By reading this book you've shown that you're looking for ways to improve your life, so continue to press on toward the victory.

Throughout this book you have discovered many ways to improve your financial condition and change your outlook on money. You may feel that you still have a long way to go, but as you continue to make progress in your financial goals be assured that God will be with you every step of the way. "Now to him who is able to do immeasurably more than all we ask or imagine, according to his power that is at work within us, to him be glory in the church and in Christ Jesus throughout all generations, for ever and ever! Amen" (Eph. 3:20–21).

Useful Web Sites

AAA: www.aaa.com

American Association of Fundraising Council: www.aafrc.org (charities)

Accuquote: www.accuquote.com (insurance)

A.M. Best Co.: www.ambest.com (insurance)

American Savings Education Council: www.asec.org (nonprofit seeking to promote personal financial independence)

Attorneyfind: www.attorneyfind.com (legal advice)

Bankrate.com: www.bankrate.com (consumer finance marketplace)

Better Business Bureau Wise Giving Alliance: www.give.org (charities)

Better Investors, magazine of the National Association of Investors: www.better-investing.org (investing)

Bloomberg L.P.: www.bloomberg.com (financial news)

Business Week Online: www.businessweek.com (financial news)

Consumer Credit Counseling Services: www.cccsintl.org (credit counseling)

Cheapskate Monthly: www.cheapskatemonthly.com (financial newsletter)

Choose to Save: www.choosetosave.org (financial education)

Christian Financial Planner Directory: www.christianfpi.org (financial planners)

CNNMoney: www.cnnmoney.com (financial news)

Consumer Federation of America: www.consumerfed.org (consumer protection)

Consumerinfo.com: www.consumerinfo.com (credit reports)

Crosswalk.com: www.crosswalk.com (online Christian community)

Crown Financial Ministries: www.crown.org (Christian financial ministry)

DaveRamsey.com: www.daveramsey.com (Christian financial ministry)

The Dollar Stretcher: www.stretcher.com (financial advice)

Entrepreneur: www.entrepreneur.com (small business advice)

Equifax: www.equifax.com (credit reports)

Evangelical Council for Financial Accountability: www.ecfa.org (charities)

Experian: www.experian.com (credit reports)

Federal Deposit Insurance Corp.: www.fdic.gov (banking)

Federal Trade Commission: www.ftc.gov (enforces consumer protection laws)

Financial Muse: www.financialmuse.com (finance for women)

Firstgov.org: www.firstgov.org (U.S. government web portal)

Hotjobs: www.hotjobs.com (careers)

Department of Housing and Urban Development: www.hud.gov (housing)

Independent Means Inc.: www.independentmeans.com (financial education for girls)

Insure.com: www.insure.com (insurance)

Investorguide.com: www.investorguide.com (investing)

Internal Revenue Service: www.irs.gov (taxes)

ivillage.com: www.ivillage.com (women's interest)

Junkbusters: www.junkbusters.com (stop junkmail and telemarketing)

Kiplinger's: www.kiplinger.com (financial news)

LendingTree: www.lendingtree.com (loans)

LowerMyBills.com: www.lowermybills.com (loans)

Mapping Your Future: www.mapping-your-future.org (financial and career planning for students and parents)

Market Watch: www.marketwatch.com (finiancial news)

MSN Money: www.moneycentral.msn.com (financial news)

MotleyFool: www.motleyfool.com (financial news and investing)

MsMoney.com Inc.: www.msmoney.com (finance for women)

MyCoupons: www.mycoupons.com (coupons and shopping)

MyMommyBiz: www.mymommybiz.com (advice for work-at-home moms)

National Database of Nonprofit Organizations:
www.guidestar.org (charities)

National Foundation for Credit Counseling:
www.nfcc.org (credit counseling)

Nolo: www.nolo.com (legal information)

PowerHomeBiz.com: www.powerhomebiz.com (small business information)

Prepaid Legal Servies Inc.: www.prepaidlegal.com (legal advice)

Privacy.org: www.privacy.org (privacy information)

Quicken: www.quicken.com (financial software and tools)

Refunding Makes Cents: www.refundcents.com (newsletter)

SelectQuote Insurance Services: www.selectquote.com (insurance)

Smart Money: www.smartmoney.com (financial news)

Social Security Administration: www.ssa.gov (social security)

Student Loan Consolidator: www.studentloanconsolidator.com (student loans)

TheStreet.com: www.thestreet.com (financial news)

Trans Union: www.transunion.com (credit reports)

U.S. Department of the Treasury: www.treasurydirect.gov (government bonds)

Women's Calendar: www.nationalwomenscalendar.org (events for women)

Women's Leadership Exchange:
www.womensleadership exchange.com (business networking)

Wall Street Journal Executive Career Site:
www.careerjournal.com (careers)

Wall Street Journal Online: www.wsj.com (financial news)

Young Money: www.youngmoney.com (finance for young adults)

Stop Telemarketing and Junk Mail

Contact the following consumer information companies and list compilers to stop junk mail and telemarketing calls.

Direct Marketing Association
Mail Preference Service
P.O. Box 643
Carmel, NY 10512
www.dmaconsumers.org (There is a $5 fee to opt out online.)

Direct Marketing Association
Telephone Preference Service
P.O. Box 1559
Carmel, NY 10512
www.dmaconsumers.org (There is a $5 fee to opt out online.)

National Do Not Call Registry
www.ftc.gov/donotcall

To opt out of catalog offers:

Abacus
P.O. Box 1478
Broomfield, CO 80038
(212) 655-4026

Opt-out number for three major credit bureaus:

1-888-5OPTOUT
    (1-888-567-8688)

To opt out of marketing lists based on county property records:

Dataquick
1-877-970-9171

To reduce mailings from major nationwide sweepstakes mailers:

Publishers Clearinghouse
101 Channel Dr.
Port Washington, NY 11050
1-800-645-9242

Readers Digest Sweepstakes
Readers Digest Rd.
Pleasantville, NY 10570

American Family Publishers
P.O. Box 62000
Tampa, FL 33662

Mailing list compilers:

Donnelley Marketing
Data Base Operations
416 S. Bell
Ames, IA 50010
1-888-633-4402

Major mailers of advertising flyers:

Harte-Hanks (Pennysaver or
    Potpourri)
2830 Orbiter St.
Brea, CA 92821
1-800-422-4116

Val-Pak Coupons
Send request to address on the
    envelope you receive.

Cox Direct/Carol Wright
Send request to address on the
    envelope you receive.

For more information about
    privacy, contact the Privacy
    Rights Clearinghouse at 619-
    298-3396 or www. privacy
    rights.org.

Financial Companies

American Express
1-800-297-5300
www.americanexpress.com

Ameritrade, Inc.
1-800-454-9272
www.ameritrade.com

Charles Schwab
1-877-488-6762
www.schwab.com

Dreyfus
1-888-271-4994
www.dreyfus.com

E*Trade
1-800-387-2331
www.etrade.com

Fidelity Investments
1-800-343-3548
www.fidelity.com

Merrill Lynch
1-877-653-4732
www.mldirect.ml.com

Sharebuilder
1-866-SHRBLDR
  (1-866-747-2537)
www.sharebuilder.com

Siebert Net
www.murielsiebert.com
1-800-872-0444

Vanguard Group
1-877-662-7447
www.vanguard.com

Notes

Day 1

1. Melvin Croan, "Berlin Wall," World Book Online Americas Edition, www.aolsvc.worldbook.aol.com/ar?/na/ar/co/ar056660.htm, September 16, 2002.

2. Annette Wirth and Frank Pawassar, "At Brandenburg Gate, Police From East and West Protect the Wall," *Die Welt*, November 13,1989, 5.

Day 2

1. Bill Hybels and Mark Mittelberg, *Becoming a Contagious Christian* (Grand Rapids: Zondervan, 1994), 57.

Day 4

1. Risa Brim, "Kids Balance Books and Money," *Lexington Herald-Leader*, March 18, 2002, C1.

Day 5

1. Andrew Backover, "A Nickel Here, a Buck There Add Up to Big Local Bills," *USA Today*, www.usa today.com/money/industries/telecom/2003-02-27-phones_x.htm, February 27, 2003.

Day 6

1. "Mail Monitor Reports Record Six Billion Credit Card Offers Mailed in U.S. During 2005," Synovate, www.synovate.com/current/news/article/2006/04/mail-monitor-174-reports-record-six-billion-credit-card-offers-mailed-in-u-s-during-2005.html, April 27, 2006.

Day 7

1. As quoted in *The Columbia World of Quotations* (New York: Columbia University Press, 1996), www.bartleby.com/66/, March 6, 2003.

2. "Show Me the Money: The State PIRGs and CFA," The PIRGS and Consumer Federation of America, www.pirg.org/reports/consumer/payday/showmethemoneyfinal.pdf, February 2000, 3.

3. Paul Laurence Dunbar, "The Debt," *The Complete Poems of Paul Laurence Dunbar* (New York: Dodd, Mead, and Co., 1913), facsimile in *The Collected Poetry of Paul Laurence Dunbar*, ed. Joanne M. Braxton (Charlottesville and London: University Press of Virginia, 1993), 213.

Day 8

1. Lukas I. Alpert, "Internet Panhandling Rescues Binge Buyer," *Associated Press*, November 5, 2002.

2. "Consumer Credit," Federal Reserve Statistical Release, http://www.federalreserve.gov/releases/g19/current/default.htm, April 7, 2006.

Day 9

1. Jay Macdonald, "Gender Spender: Sex Sets Your Money DNA," Bank rate.com, www.bankrate.com/elink/news/sav/20000620.asp?print=on, June 20, 2002.

2. "Women & Investing," Oppenheimer Funds Inc., May 9, 2002.

3. Ibid.

Day 10

1. Ana M. Aizcorbe, Arthur B. Kennickell, and Kevin B. Moore, "Recent Changes in U.S. Family Finances: Evidence from the 1998 and 2001 Survey of Consumer Finances," Federal Reserve Board, www.federal reserve.gov/pubs/bulletin/2003/0103lead.pdf, 6.

Day 11

1. S. Kathi Brown, "Impact of Stock Market Decline on 50-70 Year Old Investors," AARP, www.aarp.org/press/2002/nr121702.html, December 2002.

2. "The 2002 Retirement Confidence Survey Summary of Findings," Employee Benefit Research Institute, American Savings Education Council,

and Mathew Greenwald & Associates, Inc., www.ebri.org/res/2002/riafs
.pdf2002, 2002, 3.

3. Ibid., 11.

4. Noshua Watson, "Generation Wrecked," *Fortune*, October 14, 2002,
183.

5. "Women and Retirement Savings," U.S. Department of Labor, www
.dol.gov/ebsa/Publications/women.html, March 24, 2003.

6. "Top 10 Ways to Beat the Clock and Prepare for Retirement," U.S.
Department of Labor, www.dol.gov/ebsa/publications/10_ways_to_prepare
.html, March 24, 2003.

Day 12

1. Pat Regnier and Joan Caplin, "Can We Fix the 401(?)," *Money*, April
2003, 89.

2. Ibid.

Day 13

1. Rick Bragg, "All She Has, $150,000, Is Going to a University," *New
York Times*, August 13, 1995, A1.

2. "Giving USA 2005," Giving USA Foundation™, AAFRC Trust for
Philanthropy, http://www.aafrc.org/gusa/chartbytype.html, May 26, 2006.

Day 14

1. "Women & Investing," Oppenheimer Funds Inc., May 9, 2002.

Day 16

1. Alan Goldstein, "Online Banking Finally Clicks; More Consumers
Make Transfer to Electronic Convenience," *Dallas Morning News*, January
16, 2002, 3D.

2. Catherine Siskos, "Cash in a Flash," *Kiplinger's Personal Finance*,
October 2002, 30.

Day 17

1. Patricia Sellers, "The Business of Being Oprah," *Fortune*, www. fortune
.com, March 17, 2002.

2. Thomas J. Stanley and William D. Danko, *The Millionaire Next Door*
(New York: Pocket Books, 1996), 9.

3. Niala Boodhoo, "Americans Under 35 Savings Lag Older, Poorer Groups," *Reuters*, May 13, 2002.

Day 18

1. Glenn Kessler, "IRS Paid $30 Million in Credits for Slavery," *Washington Post*, April 13, 2002, A1.

2. David Cay Johnston, "I.R.S. Seeks Injunction Against Income-Tax Resister," *New York Times*, March 14, 2003, C4.

Day 20

1. John M. Broder, Robert Pear, and Milt Freudenheim, "Problems of Lost Health Benefits Is Reaching Into the Middle Class," *New York Times*, November 25, 2002, A1.

2. Chad Terhune, "Nonprofit Groups That Tout Insurance Have Hidden Links," *Wall Street Journal*, November 21, 2002, A1.

3. "Auto Insurance," Insurance Information Institute, http://www.iii.org/media/facts/statsbyissue/auto/, May 26, 2006.

Day 22

1. "Woman Fighting Dog's Inheritance to Get Hearing," *Los Angeles Times*, October 21, 1998, 2.

2. "Poodles to get $1m each in Rose Porteous' Will," *Australian Associated Press*, August 8, 1999.

Day 23

1. "Home Fires," National Fire Protection Association, http://www.nfpa.org/itemDetail.asp?categoryID=953&itemID=23071&URL=Research%20&%20Reports/Fire%20statistics/Trends, May 26, 2006.

2. "A Picture Is Worth a Thousand Words . . . ," Home Inventory Specialists, www.inventoryitnow.com/, March 2, 2003.

Day 25

1. Tahira K. Hira and Olive Mugenda, "Gender Differences in Financial Perceptions, Behaviors and Satisfaction," *Journal of Financial Planning*, February 2000, 88.

Francine L. Huff is a freelance journalist and author. She has worked at the *Wall Street Journal* as the spot news bureau chief, a news editor, and a copy editor. She also has worked for the *Boston Globe*, *Pittsburgh Press*, and *Valley News Dispatch* of Pennsylvania. Francine is a gifted motivational speaker who has conducted classes and workshops on finances, careers, and journalism. She has appeared on a variety of TV and radio shows, including *Crown Financial's Money Matters*, *Family Net's At Home Live*, *Good Morning Texas*, and *HomeWord With Jim Burns*. She lives in New Jersey with her husband, Gregory, and daughter, Julia. Visit her web site at www.huffwrites.com.